SHADOW ALCHEMY

JESSICA VERRILL   SAFRIANNA LUGHNA
IKENNA LUGHNA   AURELIA CORVINUS
SUSAN BENNETT FISHER   MICHELLE HAMADY
RAELEEN CASTLE   TRACEY PEFFER   KRISTINE MCPEAK
JESSICA LOUISE (BEAL)   DAWN SULLIVAN
XERES VILLANUEVA   SHANNON LORD
DANNIE FRENCH   KELLY MOWERS   DAWN HAMILTON
KIM PAGET   SARA TALIA GIZA   RED MOONEAGLE
LINDSEY RAINWATER   PENNY SISLEY   ALEPH DRASMIN

Copyright © 2024 by House of Indigo

All rights reserved.

No part of this book may be reproduced in any form or by any electronic or mechanical means, including information storage and retrieval systems, without written permission from the author, except for the use of brief quotations in a book review.

Cover Design by Aurelia Corvinus

Disclaimer

The publisher and the authors are providing this book and its contents on an "as is" basis and make no representations or warranties of any kind with respect to this book or its contents. The publisher and the author disclaim all such representations and warranties, including but not limited to warranties of healthcare for a particular purpose.

In addition, the publisher and the author assume no responsibility for errors, inaccuracies, omissions, or any other inconsistencies herein.

The content of this book is for informational purposes only and is not intended to diagnose, treat, cure, or prevent any condition or disease. You understand that this book is not intended as a substitute for consultation with a licensed practitioner. Please consult with your own physician or healthcare specialist regarding the suggestions and recommendations made in this book.

The use of this book implies your acceptance of this disclaimer.

Disclaimer

The publisher and the author make no guarantees concerning the level of success you may experience by following the advice and strategies contained in this book, and you accept the risk that results will differ for each individual. The testimonials and examples provided in this book show exceptional results, which may not apply to the average reader, and are not intended to represent or guarantee that you will achieve the same or similar results.

Contents

Foreword	9
Introduction	13
Shadow Alchemy	19
1. RECLAIMING MY WINGS Safrianna Lughna	21
Safrianna Lughna	35
2. WRITING MY OWN SCRIPT Kelly Mowers	37
Kelly Mowers	51
3. THE MOUNTAIN LION'S GRUMBLE Dawn Hamilton	52
Dawn Hamilton	59
4. FROM TRAUMA TO TRUST Sara Talia Giza	60
Sara Talia Giza	71
5. CAVERNA Dawn Sullivan	72
Dawn Sullivan	81
6. WEAVING MAGIC IN THE SHADOWS TO CREATE HARMONY BETWEEN LIGHT AND DARK Michelle Hamady	82
Michelle Hamady	95
7. THE JOURNEY TO WHOLENESS Penny Sisley	97
Penny Sisley	109
8. A CINDERELLA STORY Kim Paget	110
Kim Paget	121
9. DEATH AND LIFE/SHADOW AND LIGHT Red MoonEagle	122

Red MoonEagle	133
10. MOTHERHOOD: AN EVOLUTIONARY SPIRITUAL CONTAINER Dannie French	135
Dannie French	149
11. MIRROR MIRROR, LOOKING BACKWARD TO SEE FORWARD Kristine "Unique" McPeak	151
Kristine "Unique" McPeak	161
12. THE PEARL IN FIRE Aleph Drasmin	163
Aleph Drasmin	175
13. HOW ART CAUSED ME TO FACE THE SHADOW OF PERFECTIONISM Ikenna Lughna	176
Ikenna Lughna	185
14. LIGHT MASTERY Jessica Louise (Beal)	186
Jessica Lousie (Beal)	197
15. ECHOES OF RESILIENCE: A STORY OF RECOVERY AND RESISTANCE Xeres Villanueva	199
Xeres Villanueva	207
16. REBIRTH Shannon Lord	208
Shannon Lord	217
17. THE WAY BACK Susan Bennett Fisher	218
Susan Bennett Fisher	227
18. FINDING MY INNER COMPASS Tracey Peffer	228
Tracey Peffer	235
19. EMBRACING SHADOWS, RADIATING LIGHT Raeleen Castle	236
Raeleen Castle	243

20. SHAKTI HAS NO SHADOW: EMBRACING
    YOUR ENTIRE BEING   244
    Aurelia Corvinus

    Aurelia Corvinus   249

21. DARK FIRE RISING: MY JOURNEY TO
    SOVEREIGNTY   250
    Lindsey Rainwater

    Lindsey Rainwater   261

22. INTEGRATION   262
    Jessica Verrill

    Jessica Verrill   269
    Body of 9 Shadow Alchemy Appendix   271
    About the Publisher   285

Foreword

How do we know that we are important, that we matter?

We are born whole, perfect, with our connection to source still intact—you can see and experience it in newborn infants. In the first three months or so of life, our awareness of our source connection blurs and dissipates. Yet, that perfection, that purity of who we are, and our purpose still resides within the core of our being. When we find it, it flowers, the aroma permeating our world, the beauty reminding us of the magic we hold within us and the delicacy underscoring the importance of our offering.

Then life happens and our experiences begin to shape beliefs and survival strategies within us that obscure our view of ourselves and our value. Nurture through our life, from our parents, teachers, society, strangers, passersby, lovers, and children, all layers on top of our personal magic further obscuring our access to it. It shackles our being by creating a shadow that obscures our vision of our true selves. We spend the rest of our life journey working on becoming whole again without realizing how easy the answer to wholeness is— it's within us, who we are in our nature. It's all there, ready to go.

Shadow is created by obscuring the path of light. Shift either the light source or the obstruction, and the shadow changes, shifts or goes away completely. It is such a powerful metaphor for understanding both the challenge and the potential ease of growth and change. Shadow within us is not darkness or evil or something that is fundamentally wrong with us. Often, it is a function of a deep-seated belief developed from our life experiences to which we have attached, that obscures our ability to see other perspectives, casting what we perceive as a shadow within us.

The good news here is that once this is understood, the path to wholeness becomes illuminated. Once we realize that life is a series of choices, it allows us to observe and choose to create consciousness about our belief systems. This opens the possibility to shift the obstructions, change the light source, and even eliminate shadows. We can examine our beliefs, behaviors, and choices, then begin to create new habits and open to new possibilities.

Our life's journey then becomes one of finding our way back to that purity to give the gift that we have to offer. What if we could hold onto that perfection that comes in with us at birth, nurture our core nature as we grow and develop and not have to lose track of ourselves in order to be forced to grow?

This book is full of stories about the many ways people have found to do that. Their perspectives come from the combination of their nature and their nurture. What they have in common is courage and resiliency. To help you make sense of the varied perspectives and pick the wisdom out of their presentations, in my chapter and several of the others, context is shared on how to accelerate the process, remove the obfuscation caused by trauma, and reveal your nature.

Some of what we will describe is the Body of 9 and the Natural Numbers. There are nine physiologically different kinds of people, nine Natural Numbers as we call them at Body of 9, Inc. This is a powerfully researched discovery presented on our website Body-of9.com. It offers a context of understanding and a body-based way to rediscover the whole and essential part of who we are. This is critical to the recovery process— the process of learning to shift the light to change the angle or presence of the shadow, to see things "in a new light." The goal here is to spark curiosity in you about who you are at the level of your nature—find out your Natural Number and accelerate your own journey to wholeness, happiness, and fulfillment.

Your Natural Number provides a foundational understanding that can allow all other techniques and methods to be more easily integrated into your body, and, therefore, your life. The gifts that come with your Natural Number are given, whether with consciousness or without. Each author here is offering you the natural gifts that come with their body.

Read with an open mind and a quiet judge to receive the gifts they are offering. The authors' commitment to this project is rooted in their sincere desire to support you in discovering and nurturing your own truth. Through their stories and suggested practices, they invite you to look beyond your surface to the core of your being, where your unique strengths and talents reside.

As you read, remember that caring for yourself and your body is paramount. Approach each page with curiosity and compassion, allowing yourself space to grow and transform. Self-awareness and empowered wholeness require courage, resilience, and continued learning.

Let this book be your guide, companion, and inspiration as you uncover the magic of alchemy within you.

Susan Bennett Fisher

Introduction

When Jess Verill and I agreed to collaborate on this book together, we had no idea what we were getting ourselves into. As authors, book enthusiasts, and those quite familiar with editing, formatting, and the publication process, we *intellectually* knew what would be involved. But, we didn't realize how much of an initiation this project would be—how much *shadow alchemy* all of us would undergo in the process of creating this volume you now hold in your hands.

From deaths in families to illness to the loss of social profiles, and, quite frankly, a whole lot of dancing with daily discomforts, this project brought all the shadows to the surface. Each of us was initiated into a deeper level of self-awareness, empowerment, and liberation. Through all the ups and downs, we stood together. We cheered each other on. We processed the tough feelings. We kept going.

That's what we're here to encourage you to do.

If you've picked up this book, my guess is you're no stranger to the shadows in your life. You have likely experienced your own traumas and trials that you're still processing, or you may be going through a difficult time, even now.

We're here to let you know you are not alone.

Introduction

This book was co-created not as just a project but as a healing movement. It is a collective of voices rising together, each of us sharing stories and activities meant to liberate this world from suffering. It's time to shift our relationship with the shadows, claiming them or clearing them.

While society has tried to make us afraid of the shadows, teaching us that the "dark" things are to be avoided at all costs, my fellow collaborative authors and I would disagree. We've found the sacredness, the wisdom, and the profound transformation that's possible when we look into the shadowy parts of ourselves and uncover our nature beneath our nurture.

Healing is possible for us all–and we don't need to force or ignore it. We can find balance.

While some of the content can be heavy, *Shadow Alchemy* is a book intended to uplift, inspire, and spark conversations about topics we've often kept hidden. Our authors share insights from their personal experiences and strategies they've learned in their own journeys–from advanced teachings in energetics, mindset, and intuitive techniques, to the mundane and magical.

In each chapter, you'll find the gems excavated from each of our diverse author's shadows. They all offer practices to bring yourself into greater alignment or exploration–from journal prompts and self-reflection practices to art and visualization. You can expect to read about challenging topics like near-death experiences, recovering from abuse, and overcoming adversity and limitations. Know that each story shared comes with hope and immense wisdom–the gifts of these shadows.

You may be gently challenged as you read. You may need to put the book down a time or two. All of this is okay. The more compassionate you are as you embrace the entirety of your experience, the more you can experience this life-changing practice of alchemy.

This workbook invites you to dance between shadow and light. You will be called to tune into the often unexplored potential of your shadows, the sanctuary of inner truths just waiting to be acknowledged and understood.

Go gently on this journey. We are all here in spirit, holding the highest vision for your health and well-being, and love for the whole world.

Now, let's begin!

What is Shadow?

Shadow and light represent polarized forces or opposites. The shadow is ultimately the unseen and unconscious aspects of life.

Societally, the shadow is seen as the parts of ourselves we choose to repress or hide—the undesirable parts. Many people want to eradicate, ignore, or bypass the shadow because it can feel uncomfortable or unsightly. Yet, the shadow contains a complex blend of the suppressed and overlooked aspects of yourself, that, when embraced, offer a pathway to wholeness of Self.

Contrary to popular belief, your shadow isn't your enemy. Judgment is the real issue! Yes, this unseen side of us contains the secret vault of our fears, insecurities, and past traumas; but, it's not all negative. It can also contain repressed parts of our nature and our unknown potential just waiting to be given attention. When we are brave enough to work with our shadows, we step into the authenticity of the totality of our being, including everything we're not allowing ourselves to be.

The shadow informs not only our pain points but also our deepest yearnings. Acknowledging your shadow exists can help you receive the ultimate road map to your true self. When you dance in and out of shadow and light, you continually bring new and exciting aspects of yourself forward to be played with and explored.

What is Alchemy?

Historically, the word "alchemy" finds its roots in a blend of philosophies and practices from ancient Egypt, Greece, and medieval Europe.

The alchemists of old were often viewed as the forerunners of modern chemistry, but their work was deeply spiritual. They aimed not just to transmute base metals into gold, but also to achieve the miracle of transforming the human soul.

In alchemy, nothing is lost; everything is transformed. This is based on the principle of exchange, a foundational belief that each action incurs a reaction–a giving and receiving.

Alchemy teaches us that transformation is never a one-way process–it's an exchange with the Universe or a dialogue with the Self.

Alchemy is the art of transformation.

What is Shadow Alchemy?

Shadow Work + Energetic Alchemy = SHADOW ALCHEMY

At its core, shadow alchemy is the practice of turning the *base ingredient*—our fears, doubts, and insecurities—into metaphorical *gold*, the invaluable assets of wisdom, courage, and resilience.

When we engage in shadow alchemy, we aren't erasing or disregarding our fears and pain; we're shining a light on them so we may transmute them. We exchange shame for self-compassion, ignorance for understanding, and stagnation for growth.

Shadow alchemy isn't a one-time event but an ongoing process and spectrum of strategies that honor the complexity of human experience. It can manifest through mindfulness practices, where you sit with your darker emotions and fears to understand them better. It can occur during deep journaling sessions, where you map out the contours of your internal landscape. It might even happen in social settings, where confrontation with others reveals the shadowy aspects we usually keep hidden.

We have many alchemical practices to choose from, such as journaling, therapy, coaching, movement, or other self-development. When we use these practices intentionally, the base metals of our psyche—those elements we consider low or unworthy—become the gold of wisdom, inner peace, and self-empowerment. The most potent process, however, is consistent compassionate reflection and integration.

Introduction

In embracing shadow alchemy, we marry two seemingly separate elements—our darkest fears and our most enlightening hopes—into a harmonious, powerful whole. We don't just understand ourselves better; we also better understand the interconnectedness of light and dark, of action and consequence, of pain and healing.

How can you begin applying this concept in your life today?

What messages have you received from others or society that have made you afraid to speak your truth or use your voice?

What would change in your life if you were fully connected to the power of your voice and truth?

As you move through the stories and activities in this book, you will be invited to see yourself vulnerably, openly, and compassionately. You're invited to view your shadows not as adversaries but rather as beloved allies on your journey of self-discovery and empowerment. By embracing the full spectrum of who you are and who you came here to be, you pave the path for a life of greater harmony, purpose, and soul-level joy.

I see you. I believe in you. And, I'm cheering you on.

Safrianna Lughna
The Queer-Spirit Guide

Designed by Kim Paget

ONE

Reclaiming My Wings

Safrianna Lughna

Burying My Wings

"If you ever tell anyone about this, your mother and sister will end up dead in a ditch," said the Reaper.

This white "reborn" Christian man, more than three times my age, was going to murder my family if I spoke up about what he was doing to me. The Reaper was the puppet master of my youth.

So, of course, I stayed silent.

Starting when I was only 8 years old, his grooming and molestation escalated from occasionally, to every terrifying weekend, and then nearly daily at its peak. He manipulated me using our obvious power differences as a father figure in my life, and frequent positive reinforcement. He bought me toys, collectibles, the latest tech, and all the school supplies I wanted to create the projects I dissociated into for school. As a child who grew up in poverty, skipping meals and going without clothes that fit, it was a devious tactic to make it seem like he was actually *helping* me.

However, as I got older and began to question what was happening, he escalated to making threats. His descriptions of the harm that would come to my family sliced through me like scythes– my soul retreating to stay safe. Protective "Parts" of me, my own

Knights-in-Shining-Armor, charged forward to save my loved ones from impending danger. If I didn't stay quiet, they'd face the Reaper in a more deadly way than I.

Before the shadow of the Reaper crept into my life, I resonated with the concept of having wings. I could feel my invisible wings supporting me whenever I leaped from branch to branch in the maple tree that wild-mothered me. They emerged from between my shoulder blades, holding me in perfect balance: an unseen shadow to my light. I knew I was safe! My enormous, inky black wings, shimmering with stars and all the colors of the Universe, would never let me fall. These wings were proof to me that I was magical.

Then, I was extracted from my natural home in the trees and placed instead inside the den of a predator. Suffering in silence and no longer able to feel my wings, I believed the Reaper had cut them off. Yet, within the quiet of my Soul, a whisper of hope remained—unseen, but unforgotten, promising the possibility of flight one day.

Rejecting My Body

By 9 years old, I was well acquainted with days lost to dissociation. As things began to happen to my body that confused and disoriented me, I escaped upwards. It was a different sort of flight–the detached, out-of-control swirl of trauma and torture.

In the same months the sexual abuse began, I started experiencing hallucinations. Terrifying visions manifested before my open eyes, warning me of the danger I was in. Static TV screens would blink on as my mind drifted toward what was happening to me. Spiked walls closed in when my body began to fight back with fevers to process the harm the Reaper was inflicting. Once as I was hiding in the bathroom, I saw a bloody child in the bathtub who warned me I would die.

Terror followed me everywhere, and I had no idea how to express or process any of it. I was not safe anywhere–not with peers, not with authority figures, and certainly not with the people in my own home.

The Reaper taught me I was an object to be used by adult men.

Sexuality wasn't something empowering or enjoyable. It was a secretive thing, hidden in the shadows of the trailer parks and suburban neighborhoods I moved between every few years.

But as a budding young woman, I saw my peer's identities forming as they entered middle school. Everyone was talking about crushes; some were even "dating," and it dawned on me that such things were possible for me, too. Maybe I was more than what was happening when no one was watching.

I began to consider my own identity in the world and started to question everything. My energy began to subtly push back against the Reaper as if my Soul was daring to return to my body and reclaim my truth. Scared he'd lose his "supply" of selfish pleasure, he doubled down with threats.

I started to hate the mere idea of sexuality—I believed pleasure was never meant to be *mine*, but rather something to be harvested from me.

But that all changed when I met a girl.

Although she was two years older than me, she rode the same bus when we stayed late for after-school activities. I found the curl of her red hair charming, all the way from the cropped short top curls down to the back of her rat's tail, which fell over the collar of her anime t-shirts. Weeks later, we tumbled–kissing–onto her mother's lacey guest bed, surrounded by miniature porcelain knick-knacks.

It was an awakening! With a thrill of self-recognition, I realized my confusing crush on Aladdin *and* Jasmine translated to real life, too.

I thought I was in love. We traded notes whenever we could, sometimes passing between a mutual friend. But, it was too good– and pure–to last.

When the Reaper found out, he was furious. He searched through my backpack and found our latest confessions of love and longing to see each other.

It disgusted him.

During the '90s and 2000s, anti-gay and queerphobic comments were the norm. Being gay was a punchline, if not an actual excuse to physically or sexually assault someone.(1) While I didn't know it at the time, I could feel it: I was in danger.

The Reaper, red-faced, said, "This is sin. You are a girl. You can't be with a girl. You will go straight to Hell." Shaking his head, he looked at me as if I was blind to my own foolishness.

It brought back memories of earlier childhood religious traumas–crying alone in bed, fearful that God would smite me for being somehow wrong. And here it was yet again: my wrongness.

The Reaper then delivered the words that haunted my sexuality for years: "If you tell anyone about us, I'll tell your Mother what a dirty little lesbian you are."

It'd be years before I'd realize the Reaper was gaslighting me into believing I was the problem. The true sins were committed by him–traumatizing young, impressionable me with fear and shame to keep me quiet.

But, I didn't know better then. While I continued to have secret crushes on all genders and experimented where I could, I isolated my identity down to sexual sinner, irredeemable and sacrilegious.

The Reaper's shadow covered every area of my life for years.

I stayed quiet when my best friend's older brother forced me to do things I didn't want.

I stayed quiet when a classmate assaulted me in his basement and took pictures of my tear-smudged face and crumpled body.

I stayed quiet when the man I thought was my "Twin Flame" violated all of my boundaries, repeatedly, every date night while systematically cutting me off from my friends and family.

Silencing my own feelings, desires, and dreams became my norm. I shoved them like shoe boxes in a dark basement. My own sexuality, joy, and pleasure? Exiled, seeped in sin, and buried in the same grave as my amputated wings.

Into the "Light" of Limiting Beliefs

As a result of my traumatic childhood experiences, I found my truth suffocated by limiting beliefs, self-destructive behaviors, and low self-worth. Thoughts like, "I'm not enough. I'll never be more than a sex toy," ran my life.

The day I turned 18, I tried to leave the cycle of non-stop trauma. I moved from Maryland to Tennessee, taking my beat-up car and moving in with my online boyfriend and his parents. Since he'd talked me down from another suicide attempt, I held hope I could make a happy life with him as I ran away from all the bad things that had "happened to me."

Spoiler alert: Things didn't get better.

My sexual expression came and went like damp sparklers at a drunken 4th of July bash; sporadic and rarely aligned or healthy. My relationships bounced between unfulfilling and neglectful to highly explosive and toxic, with no in-between. I was depressed, dissociated, drunk frequently, and suicidal because I had so much unprocessed trauma.

But, I was also an adult now–I needed to work, provide, and be successful. I was a woman in a man's world, the "real world" I was warned about in my youth, and I needed to fight to prove my worth. If I wanted anything out of life, I needed to be relentless in my pursuit of meeting my goals.

I consciously held these thoughts in the "light," believing them to be true. That's the thing. Just because something is visible does not necessarily make it true. Just because something is present in the light, or our conscious mind, does not make it correct. These beliefs played on repeat in my mind and were even validated by family members and partners. Yet, somewhere inside me, the embers of my Soul remained. I knew these thoughts and relationships were completely out of alignment, toxic, and consuming me alive. Their version of success wasn't mine.

We have to assess our inner narratives from time to time because when they're out of alignment, they don't just harm us. They can impact how we see and treat other people. We're constantly projecting our inner world outward.

For decades, I believed myself unworthy of healthy relationship dynamics, peace, and ease. I held that I was at the mercy of men and a patriarchal society. I believed the only way to make it in the world was to hustle, grind, push, and force my way to "success." I felt the only answers were outside of me, and I needed to follow the advice of authorities, coaches, and gurus who "knew the secrets to a better life."

My unpleasant wake-up call for change came when I recognized one of my long-term relationships was a textbook case of intimate partner violence, shades of my dynamics with the Reaper. As my eyes opened, I understood the ways I was harming myself. I was holding tightly to the idea I must save others or be a salve for their wounds. I allowed myself to be violated because I believed that was what I deserved and that it would help others heal.

I was repeating patterns of trauma from my childhood and generations of my family before me. By ignoring my exiled Parts and memories, I lacked the ownership and awareness needed to liberate myself from victim mentality. The heaviness of negative self-talk, people-pleasing, masking, and constant hypervigilance were like lead weights in my pockets. While I carried them, I knew I would never fly.

These beliefs and cycles were no longer mine. I knew I deserved better beliefs and a more empowered life, as do we all.

Changing My Patterns

As I realized I was not meant to fix or save others, I simultaneously understood I must have some other mission here on Earth. I decided to explore my shadows to find my truth. I retreated into my own reprocessing chrysalis to rediscover the seeds of who I came here to be. I unpacked the ways I was conditioned to patterns of people-pleasing, minimizing, self-sacrifice, silence, and dissociation.

It is not through ignoring our experiences of pain or suffering that we become joyful, content, and well-balanced people. It is through witnessing and learning to love every single Part of ourselves, especially those who have experienced life-altering circumstances. This is *shadow alchemy*.

Through years of therapy, Shamanic healing, energy work, coaching, and enough self-care modalities to fill a manual, I retrieved lost Parts of me fragmented from decades of trauma. I uncovered my own unique process of *shadow alchemy* to unhook from the false stories. By examining my beliefs, behaviors, and choices in an empowered way, I excavated the truth of my own emotions, desires, dreams, pleasures, creativity, and inner fire. I initiated the process of reclaiming myself. I committed to my truth.

I brought myself home.

I am not my traumas, nor am I stuck on a loop repeating them. When I make it a priority to look at, feel, and explore the emotions and Parts of myself impacted by traumatic events, I stay whole within the dance of life. This allows me to create a balance between healing and playing, creating and feeling—moving in and out of shadow and light.

In the darkest places of my subconscious, I found my voice and wings again. They were there all along, just hidden deep inside so that I could claim them when I was ready to soar again. In this reclamation, I've discovered that the greatest power lies not in avoiding the darkness, but in using it as the backdrop against which the stars of our deepest truths shine brightest.

Although I have recovered my wings, I am still learning the art of flying. Over thirty years after my first sexual trauma, I still find myself plucking out barbs of codependent behaviors and self-silencing that keep me from ascending as high as I can.

I cannot save anyone or control anything—other than myself. I anchor into this truth over and over so I can make sovereign decisions and hold sacred my aligned vision and embodied blueprint.

My sexuality and spirituality are my own. I am here to be me, to express myself authentically, and to enjoy the pleasures of this life. Shadow alchemy allowed me to embrace this truth.

Flying Freely Through Shadow and Light

This is a world of polarity, magnetism, spectrums with defined extremes, and a whole lot of room for balance. We've become so out of alignment that we're overcompensating too much in extreme directions. We avoid, suppress, shame, blame, and ignore.

Contrary to the popular narrative, the shadow is not bad. Sure, it's not all comfortable, but when integrated, it is empowering.

I invite you to process through your triggers and experiences of trauma in your own way. In doing so, you increase our capacity to:

- Hold your own aligned consciousness and unconsciousness
- Balance doing and being
- Give and receive
- Create and enjoy
- Harmonize your inner light (solar) and shadow (lunar) energy

When we can move in and out of light and shadow, comfort and discomfort, seen and unseen, we find more unity and flow within ourselves.

Healing is a lifelong process. But, it doesn't have to be *hard* or *constant*. Allow yourself a calm and compassionate space to get curious. Examine your triggers, challenging memories, unsupportive patterns, and any harmful beliefs hiding within you.

Each day gets to be a journey upward when you remember to love yourself. This is the dance of post-traumatic growth, returning to self-empowerment, love, and trust. We weave in and out of light and shadow, retrieving wisdom from both sides and integrating them together.

The interplay of shadow and light mirrors the wings we each possess—without both, flying free in life remains a dream. Embrace your full spectrum: it's in the harmony of these forces that we unlock our true potential.

It's time to claim your truth, your light and shadow, unfurling both wings to soar. Now is the moment to rise, transcend limitations, and embrace the boundless sky of possibility. It's time to be you.

The Spectrum of Energetic Harmony to Disharmony *by Safrianna Lughna*	
Harmony	
The Aligned Light	The Aligned Shadow
<ul><li>Balanced, compassionate giving</li><li>Empowered aligned actions</li><li>Mindfulness, presence</li><li>Embodiment</li><li>Self-expression</li></ul>	<ul><li>Boundaried, grateful receiving</li><li>Willingness to engage with feelings and inner experiences</li><li>Exploring Soul-level desires</li><li>Constructive self-reflection</li></ul>
Neutrality	
Light (Neutral Energy)	Shadow (Neutral Energy)
<ul><li>Illuminated Space</li><li>Conscious</li><li>Active Healing</li><li>Engagement</li><li>Intellect</li><li>Solar Energy (Masculine / Masc)</li></ul>	<ul><li>Unseen Space</li><li>Subconscious</li><li>Subtle/passive healing</li><li>Imagination</li><li>Intuition</li><li>Lunar Energy (Feminine / Femme)</li></ul>
Disharmony	
The Unaligned Light	The Unaligned Shadow
<ul><li>Wounded conscious beliefs</li><li>Overdoing or over-functioning</li><li>Intellectualization of feelings</li><li>Demanding others be a part of our vision for how to "be" and "do" ("I'm right.")</li><li>Being performative</li><li>Over-identification with roles</li><li>Spiritual bypassing</li><li>Hero complexes and martyrdom</li></ul>	<ul><li>Wounded subconscious beliefs</li><li>Disconnection or under-functioning</li><li>Repressed desires and emotions</li><li>Overidentification with feelings</li><li>Fear and insecurity ("I am wrong.")</li><li>Trauma stories, limiting beliefs, and wounds</li><li>Unconscious motivations</li><li>Victim mentality</li></ul>

Reclaiming Your Wings: An Alchemical Process

Everything comes back to our relationship with our core Self, our Soul. To me, we "fly" when we are self-empowered, awake, and compassionate towards ourselves. This means holding space for both our shadow and our light, navigating from disharmony to harmony.

To foster more self-empowerment and alignment, we need to cultivate:

- **Self-Awareness**: Acknowledging that your shadows (or disharmonized light) exist.

- **Self-Ownership**: Take responsibility for these shadow Parts of you. They are there; they are yours.

- **Self-Acceptance**: Understand that these shadow Parts are also aspects of your wholeness.

- **Self-Love**: Embrace these wounded Parts of you. Love them. It's through love that the healing transformation occurs.

I invite you to explore each component through journaling or reflection and unpack how you can step into more alignment as you reclaim your wings and voice.

Self-Awareness

Reflect on a recent moment when you felt triggered or uncomfortable. Describe the situation, your reaction, and the emotions it stirred within you. What do you think this reaction says about your inner shadows or disharmonized light? How can acknowledging this shadow help you understand yourself better?

Self-Ownership

Identify a shadow part of yourself that you've recognized. Write about how this part has influenced your decisions and relationships. Then, consciously take responsibility for this part by declaring it as yours. How does owning this aspect of yourself change your perception of its impact on your life?

Self-Acceptance

Consider the shadow part of yourself that you've been working to own. Explore ways in which this shadow contributes to your wholeness and personal growth. What strengths or lessons has it brought you, even indirectly? How can you integrate this understanding into a broader acceptance of yourself?

Self-Love

Write a letter of love and compassion to the shadow part you've identified and begun to accept. Address it directly, expressing understanding, forgiveness, and unconditional love. What promises can you make to this part of yourself to ensure it feels seen, valued, and integrated into your being?

Claiming Your Empowered Flight

Now, let's reclaim those wings! Reflect on situations where you have felt free, empowered, and/or joyful. On each feather, write down a strength or gift you have, a support or tool you use, or a passion that lifts you up. Then, you can consider how to integrate these elements more fully into your day-to-day life.

Reclaiming My Wings

Safrianna Lughna

Safrianna Lughna, LCPC, M.S., is the Queer-Spirit Guide: a freely flying beacon of alignment, authenticity, and empowerment. With her unique blend of experience as a public school teacher, trauma therapist, and cheerleader for the "weird" and "woo," Safrianna weaves magic into all she creates. As an author, speaker, CEO, and guide, she supports visionary leaders and healers seeking to own their truth and magnify their impact for a better world.

At the heart of her mission is her business, Living LUNA: a podcast, community, and initiative for social change. Safrianna creates spaces of sanctuary for those often deemed "Others." Whether guiding one-on-one sessions, crafting transformative ritual and retreat experiences, or leading the Living LUNA movement, Safrianna approaches life with sparkle, curiosity, and compassion.

Safrianna treasures the art of self-care—penning poetry and science fiction, diving into thought-provoking video games, and enjoying moments with her polycule and cats. She is a Natural Number 9; 6/2 Manifesting Generator; a Gemini Sun and Cancer Moon, with a North Node in Aquarius, for those playing along.

You're invited to join Safrianna on this journey of discovery and empowerment, where every step off the well-worn societal path is a step toward your true self.

Discover more and join the flight:
Websites: https://LivingLUNAs.com | https://Safrianna.com
YouTube: https://www.youtube.com/@LivingLUNA
Living LUNA Discord Community: https://discord.me/livingluna

(1) According to numerous studies released over the past several decades, LGBTQIA+ and especially bisexual girls and women are abused at statistically higher numbers than other populations (even higher for trans feminine people). See LivingLUNAs.com/statistics for more information.

TWO

Writing My Own Script

Kelly Mowers

(Fast Forward to:)
Creativity and Chaos (cont'd)

Act 2, Scene 2: Last year of Graduate School (twenty-five years ago) The MFA in Creative Writing program.

KELLY
(Speaking to the audience.)

In this craziness of creativity and chaos, I embrace my crazy. I really am an alien or a Starseed. I am who I am. I am here on a mission. What was lost now is found. The Knowing and soft voices are back. I feel I am one of the sanest in this sea of insanity.

I begin to sink into the deep darkness of experimentation, drinking, and automatic writing. If you write something effortlessly, and it is pretty damn good, but you don't remember writing it, did you write it? Who wrote it? Or if you are receiving downloads of information and writing what you are receiving, is it your writing? I am awakening to all that we are. I feel this openness. This love for everyone. This connection to everyone and everything.

I am the dancing queen, wild and free—older than seventeen (Abba). I stay up all night in nightclubs. Me! I used to be shy. I am now unstoppable. I teach in the afternoons and write poems and stories into the night. I don't need sleep. I workshop and listen to everyone find brilliant things in my writing—and many negative things. I laugh. Why am I laughing?

My thesis professor asks me why my eyes are so messed up. He also asks the entire class what the hell I did to my hair, now raven black. I laugh and keep laughing until I wake up in the dark, the television light flickering *Twin Peaks* next to me. The smell of vomit all over me: a vague memory of deciding I would reach the stars and my Galactic family on my own.

(Lights go out.)

Crashing Down
Act 3, Scene 1:

Character: Call me Kellyopi (mistaken for the Greek name Calliope). The perfect Greek (yes, I ran away to Greece!) Stepford wife. Oh yeah, I am married and pregnant and seemingly pure. After all, the Greek Orthodox Bishop looked into my eyes and said I was worthy of marrying an Orthodox Greek male in an Orthodox

Church. He then told me to kiss the rings on his hand. I didn't want to, but I did. So I must be okay. Right?

My new mantra: I will be normal. I will be normal. I will be normal.

How long this version of perfection lasts: From dating to marrying to being five months pregnant: all told, about a year.

Why this illusion shattered: I lost the baby. I was pretending to be someone I wasn't. He pretended to be someone he wasn't. I lost the baby…

Scene setting: a male voice shouting into the darkness.

HUSBAND (O.S)

You are useless! You can't even have my baby.

(Kellyopi enters the stage carrying swords. She is wearing a black ripped hooded cape.)

KELLYOPI

The Three of Swords to my Heart. The Ten of Swords in my back.

(She drops swords on the stage. She sinks to her knees. The stage turns black.)

(Lights stay off while the black cape is removed and the crib is brought on stage.)

Scene setting: In a soft spotlight, Kellyopi is standing alone. She is now wearing a yellow flowered dress with a white scalloped collar. The second spotlight turns on, revealing a crib behind her. Both spotlights fade. A music box is heard while stars circle the ceiling and floor.

KELLYOPI
(Has become a recluse after suffering from a miscarriage.)

Alone in the house,
The baby cries
In the empty crib
In the darkness
The mobile of stars spins
On the ceiling
As a music box plays
My hair fans the teal marble floor as
My hands run over the empty womb
You cry and cry
But I cannot reach you
The One in Gray came
In dreams and visions
Insisting
Your name was on his list
To never breathe in
The polluted air or

Writing My Own Script

See the sunrise
The half-finished nursery
Of blue and yellow
Will never hold you
And I wish I could die
To be together
Instead of this useless
Vessel
Left here with a bathtub and a blade
Tissues and a small coffin
With clothes that are not my own
I awaken from the fog
And cut them up
I have always hated yellow flowers
The teal marble
Becomes a sea
And I float there for hours
Listening to you
In my mind
The invisible rocking chair rocks
In the corner
The doorknob turns, and
The Greek prodigy
Ordained as the family patriarch
Comes home to find me
Asleep on the floor
In the dark
Only the stars circling on the ceiling
Yelling for his food
Yelling for his wife
Both are nonexistent
He says he does not know me
That I am mad
That I am useless
He grabs the mobile from your crib
And smashes it

I will never forgive him
I am surprised that he can still see me
Because I am already dead
The front door slams
And I barely breathe
Alone
Amongst the cut-up clothes,
Broken plastic, batteries, and
Music still desperately
Trying to turn the stars
And the invisible rocking chair rocks
And you cry from a great distance
And I cannot save you…

KELLYOPI (CONT'D)

(Kellyopi pauses and begins speaking desperately to an invisible person.)

I was lost in darkness, you see. My mind was trapped. And no one speaks of miscarriages or lost babies… angel babies. So, I was alone in my grief. I quit my job as a teacher because I couldn't even look at children. I was jealous of every woman that was pregnant. I was jealous of every family that passed by. I broke into tears continuously, and no one understood why. I had no friends, and my family was far away. I was married to someone I didn't know and who couldn't understand me. I couldn't understand myself.

I was bitter and confused by his narcissism. I didn't realize the empath is like a moth that shrivels when it flies too close to the fire of the narcissist. I felt worthless. I couldn't do anything correctly. I took down the Christmas tree before Christmas. I couldn't stand the happiness of others. I was a Shadow of myself.

(Lights turn off.)

Utter Darkness of Self-Disdain
Act 3, Scene 2

Scene setting: Viewing hours. Spotlight on a coffin located center stage. Many people surround the casket. The crying goes silent when Kellyopi speaks, but the people on stage still silently act out the motions of despair. (V.O)

KELLYOPI

I am standing here at the viewing hours, the day before her funeral. I stare into the casket of my friend, or maybe I should say, my neighbor. I am not sure she would consider me her friend. I look down on a beautiful young woman who died from a brain aneurysm. I kiss her forehead and gently brush my finger on the cheek of her baby, which lies dead beside her. I am crying: tears for this tragedy and tears for my darkness. I feel pure hatred for myself.

This is the first time I confront this beast that I have become. I wonder if my pain can be heard growling over the wailing of the fainting women in black.

(Kellyopi stares at the audience and points at them:)

I see you shaking your head in confusion. You think I am sweet and kind and loving. And I am, sometimes. But you don't know my thoughts. You didn't hear my thoughts on a constant loop. You see, I was at her wedding a couple of months ago. (Pointing to her resting in the coffin.)

We were dancing and smiling, but I was so jealous of everything she had—A happy relationship and her baby girl on the way. Now, she is in a casket, cradling her baby.

Scene setting: The women begin to wail loudly. The lights gradually rest on a priest who is pacing near the door. Kellyopi puts her hands over her ears as she cries. She starts screaming the next words, returning to a normal tone as gradually the crying silences around her. (V.O.)

KELLYOPI (CONT'D)

I am crying for the loss of her beautiful soul and for the child that was days from being born. But I am also crying because I wasn't sincerely happy for her at her wedding. The Darkness in me wondered why I couldn't be that happy. It was a jealousy that smoldered, and many times, it consumed me. I wanted to have everything she had. Her genuine smile. The look of adoration her husband beamed at her. Her family and friends circling her and holding her in love. I thought how unfair it was that she had everything and I had nothing. I hugged her, smiled, and ate her cake. I drank her champagne, watching her and all the mothers dancing with their children. I smiled, but no one could have known the dark voice in my mind, thinking, "They don't deserve them; they don't love them as much as I would."

And now she is dead. Her baby is dead.

Scene setting: Suddenly, the Greek Orthodox priest walks up to the casket and tries to rip the dead baby from her lifeless arms. There is a struggle.

PRIEST

Δεν βαφτίζεται!

KELLY

He says that he cannot allow an unbaptized child to be properly buried. Everyone is yelling. Her mother faints on the floor beside me.

There is chaos.

In that moment, organized religion becomes dead to me. What religion, what God, would not allow this child into heaven?

I stop crying.

**Remembering
Act 4, Scene 1:**

Scene setting: Candles light up the darkness behind the coffin.

KELLY (CONT'D)

My anger and bitterness are replaced with needing and wanting to help those who could not help themselves. If the priest had tried again to take the child from my friend's arms, I would have been there to stop him. I think he sensed that many of us would not allow him to separate the baby from her mother. He baptized the baby right there, in her arms, within the casket. It was interesting to see him toil with what he knew to be right and what the rules of the church dictated. I felt empathy for him, whereas moments before, there had been nothing but rage.

In that darkness of grief, jealousy, and bitterness, I felt nothing but disgust for myself and others. Now I begin to remember, remember, remember. I look at the priest and see the candles flickering behind the coffin. I can see the flickers of light where there were only shadows. It is up to us to rise from the shadow to embrace the light. A cliché! We all know this, but when you are lost down there, surviving as a sliver of a human being, you cannot see the flicker of light—even if it is right in front of you.

**Lessons Learned
Act 4, Scene 2:
The last monologue:**

KELLY

I began helping refugees who were risking their lives in hopes of a better life. They still flee war and poverty every single day. They give every cent they have to put their family on rubber rafts in hopes of reaching European shores. International asylum laws promise them this chance of a new life.

"The EU is an area of protection for people fleeing persecution or serious harm in their country of origin. Asylum is a fundamental right and an international obligation for countries, as recognized in the 1951 Geneva Convention on the protection of refugees." (EU Official Website CEAS)

Yet, Europe has turned its back on this crisis. The Greek coastguard takes the engines off the boats and "pushes them back" to Turkey. They deny it, but survivors talk. The news once showed the Italians watching a sinking boat, ignoring the pleas for help while they drowned. You can Google "picture of a young Syrian boy wearing a red shirt and denim seen rocking face-down on the shoreline" to see the image that haunts my dreams. But I don't recommend it. He was three years old. Alan Kurdi. So much tragedy.

I went back to teaching and inspiring children. I went back to being me. I faced that ugly Darkness that had grown in my depression, and I transformed it into Light and Love that I now aim to radiate to everyone.

This time period in Greece represented the last time I tried to be someone else. Occasionally, I still have to hide my existence from those not ready to understand. This was the advice given by the Elder Greek women who whispered while weeping, the ones reading my Greek coffee cup and dancing under the full moon. Everything was secret! Μυστικά, μυστικά, μυστικά. Secrets, secrets, secrets from the males, the patriarchs and modern society. I learned the Pagan ways. I learned the magic of herbs, nature, and the sky. I learned to honor the Earth, Air, Water, Fire, and Spirit. I listened to languages that only some on Earth understand, languages from long ago—Tongues and Light Languages.

Through whispers, I remember my Starseed lineage. I dream of shouting through a blow horn, "I am a Starseed! Are you? There is so much more! Open your eyes, your heart." Then, those ready to hear the words awaken, slowly rubbing their eyes and seeing things for the first time. Others hug me and ask me why it took me so long to remember who I am.

And the others? They would continue to stare glossy-eyed into the matrix of their future. Being a Starseed or following the Pagan ways isn't a secret. But some are not ready to remember or open their fearful minds.

I know that a New Earth is coming. Raising our vibration or frequency all over the world is imperative. I am grateful to my Shadow, who was so lost in that dark labyrinth because it was in that darkness that I saw the flicker of light. How biblical! I truly think this is where organized religion began: it just got lost along the way.

Some say that I am a Blue Ray Starseed or Gridworker and Lightworker—I travel from place to place, radiating light and frequency that reaches into the souls of the ones lost in their darkness. Others say I am an empathic healer, a Weaver, an INFJ, a Starseed Augur, or a Natural Number 6. I might be a bit of all of these.

I don't have a single label to give myself, and I don't think I need any title to define me—I just have a Knowing of being here to help. I chose to be here—I think most of us have a dark and confusing journey to thank for the Light and Love we now emit in all directions, embracing Mother Gaia and radiating into the stars above.

Exercises

Think of a time you were wrestling with your Shadow. Where were you? How was your breathing? What could you smell? Feel? Add these thoughts to a color that you are not.

Example: I am not Yellow…

I am not the yellow-flowered dress that you insisted I wear. I am not Van Goh's ugly sunflowers hanging over my childhood bed in a room of plaid sun. Those evil flowers whispered nightmares into my ears, even with the pastel cotton sheets wrapped firmly around my head…I can still smell the decaying black stems in the cloudy water.

Now contrast that with the color you are and happier thoughts. Work through the pain and frustration of the Shadow experience through journaling, poetry, and colors:

Examples: I am not the scent of the sun but of the night budding jasmine. The delicate white petals against the dark green leaves can be found by their pleasant pure perfume on a moonless meandering.

I am Bordeaux…a fine wine of dark lipstick, leaving my essence in spirals between your legs…I am the bordeaux velvet dress that hangs off my shoulders as you kiss my neck…maroon masks masquerading under the full moon—making me more maidenlike than motherly…a cranberry craze of creativity and chaos.

Now, invite yourself to write one or two poems that use these exercises as a starting point. Try stream-of-consciousness writing—just let the ideas and images flow. Write down everything because you never know what will emerge, inspire, and heal. I hope this exercise helps you express yourself in a fun and healing way.

Kelly Mowers

Kelly Elizabeth Mowers is a writer and teacher of English for Multilingual Learners. She enjoys traveling and learning new languages and ideas. She is constantly seen carrying a book or two as she is an avid reader and spiritual seeker. She has published poetry and short stories and has won writing competitions. Her passion for helping others is seen in her volunteer work with various NGOs and with refugees in her local community.

She has a Master of Fine Arts in Creative Writing, with a concentration in teaching ESL. She hopes to publish her first book of poetry this year and has a novel or two whispering to be written in the near future.

If you have also survived the experience of pregnancy loss, Kelly invites you to reach out about possible collaborative opportunities to heal using poetry, stories, and art. You can reach her at: **kellyelizabethmowers@gmail.com**

THREE

The Mountain Lion's Grumble

Dawn Hamilton

It started out as a simple suggestion. My best friend suggested I schedule an appointment to see a massage therapist named Sandy. At the time, I didn't understand that this decision was going to change my life.

Sandy was a gifted healer. Our first session was about physical massage therapy. As I continued to work with Sandy, she began to introduce me to various healing modalities like Reiki and Craniosacral Therapy. Reiki is defined as an energy massage that assists your spiritual body. Craniosacral Therapy works on harmonizing and balancing your nervous system.

She also educated me on how to use Oracle cards and suggested books and articles for me to read. We fell into a monthly routine. We met on Wednesday evenings around the new moon each month. She taught me about the cycles and rhythms of the moon and the changes of the seasons. Over time, the monthly sessions became deeper healing work.

Slowly, without paying attention to it, my life began to change. It was subtle at first. My body began to feel better. As my life came into alignment, bigger shifts started to occur. My relationship with my husband shockingly and abruptly ended. I wasn't expecting this, and it shook the core of my foundation. Sandy and our monthly sessions helped me process this and slowly put myself back together.

She also acquainted me with another healing modality called Shamanism. Over a 10-year period, this was a catalyst for profound growth. Annually, we would get together for a Soul Retrieval ceremony. A Soul Retrieval involves working with a Shaman. The premise is attending a small group healing ceremony. The Shaman spiritually travels to retrieve and bring back suspended or fragmented pieces of your soul that are ready to be reintegrated. It was explained to me like this; "Think of your life as a beautiful pearl necklace. When trauma occurs, the necklace breaks and the pearls become separated from the string. Sometimes, the pearls fall so far away that they are not naturally brought back after the trauma. This is where the Shaman can assist in bringing back the fragmentation."

As I continued to work with Sandy, I was absolutely stunned again. This time my mother passed away unexpectedly. She was my personal cheerleader and my biggest fan. To say I was devastated was an understatement. Grief is a very hard taskmaster. At the time my mother passed away, I didn't understand grief. I was just starting to understand basic concepts of spirituality. With the shock of her death, I found myself trying to figure out how I was going to define myself.

My world continued to change. My life pivoted once again, and I found myself without a job. My career, which had become my identity, was now gone. My mother just passed away months beforehand. I was struggling to see who I was or how I fit into the world.

The universe had a surprise for me. Sandy invited me to go on a trip out West with her. Because the universe had unceremoniously rearranged my life, I found myself open to the idea. I went on an epic road trip with Sandy. We lived in her Chevy Tahoe for a month. We slept at different campsites and visited a variety of places I'd never been to.

There was one very profound experience that ultimately changed everything.

On that day, I woke up with a blinding headache. The sunlight was too much. The sound of the birds singing hurt my ears. I could barely breathe without any pain. I had a migraine of epic proportions.

I thought I was going to die. I just wanted to crawl in a hole with no light, no noise. I wanted to hide. I could barely move my body without triggering a reaction. I could feel my pulse and its banging in my brain. It felt as if each heartbeat would cause my skull to bust open any minute. I was tough, but this was unbearable, even for me.

Sandy told me that it was the day we were headed to the mine. I wasn't ready to move. At that time, I believed any movement would induce sudden death. The pain was excruciating, and I welcomed the idea. I just wanted to stop that pain.

At this point, we had been living in her Chevy Tahoe for about two weeks. The plan had always been to visit the silver mine she owned in the Nevada Mountain ranges. We were going no matter how I felt.

Sandy drove. I tried to sleep in the back. I felt each bump in the road. We made it to a grocery store so I could buy some medicine. I pulled myself out of the back of the Tahoe. The sun blinded me. I tried to count my steps, breathing slowly, doing everything within my power to not throw up.

I purchased my meds and made my way slowly back to the car. I climbed in the back of the Tahoe and realized I didn't have anything to drink. I swallowed the tablets anyway. They got stuck in my throat. My frustration level grew.

About 90 minutes later, Sandy pulled into a restaurant parking lot. We were about halfway to our destination. I extracted myself from the car. Breakfast was a quick affair. I made the conscious decision to try and behave like a human. While I was still miserable, I rode up front with Sandy. I had to try.

To get to the mine, we had to drive up a gravel road to the foothills. We started our slow ascent. Sandy was extremely cautious while driving. The air filled with dust from the moving car. It left a long visible trail behind us.

It took us about an hour to park the car. We prepared to make the rest of the transit on foot. Somehow, I finally felt better.

As we prepared for our hike, Sandy explained to me that there

The Mountain Lion's Grumble

are wild animals living in the mountains, some of them dangerous. We needed to make a lot of noise on the trail. Sagebrush grew along the path which hid all sorts of things that could bite us, so we dressed for the occasion. We donned jeans and tucked our pants in our socks. We placed spats over our hiking boots and packed food and water.

Sandy handed me two rocks and sent me up the trail. She instructed me to bang them together. I followed a rutted path up the mountain. The path was a water run-off and had the appearance of a pitted dry stream bed. Sandy asked me to bang louder and make more noise—keep moving, but not too fast.

The sun is at its apex in the sky. My hands tingle from the force of banging rocks together. Periodically the rocks break from so much banging, and I picked up more along the way.

We made a few twists and turns on the trail and finally ended up at our destination. Sandy was very excited to be there. The views were spectacular. There wasn't a cloud in the sky, and we could see for miles. We talked a bit about the silver mine, and she started showing me rocks and boulders. I learned how to spot the minerals.

After a bit, we sat to eat and hydrate. By then, I had started to feel like a new person. My behavior had changed to a more playful side. I sang goofy songs, hopped around and played.

Sandy wanted to take pictures at the opening of the mine. I waited for her to climb up, and I took her picture. We exchanged places. As she was getting ready to take the picture, I started laughing. I told her that the ground sure sounded funny up there, and I kept laughing. Sandy took my picture and asked me what I meant by that. I made a low grumble sound and laughed because I couldn't make the sound right. It sounded like a low motor being revved.

Sandy called me down. It was time to pack up and head back to the car. Sandy and I selected some large rock samples and filled the backpacks. I carried a backpack with the rocks down the trail.

Again, our descent was loud. I broke additional rocks on the way down. My voice boomed with stories, songs, and laughter as we descended. I was a different person on the way down. Even though I carried the large rocks in my backpack, I somehow felt lighter.

We returned to the Tahoe and stowed the gear and the bounty we carried. After we jumped in the car, Sandy shared a few things.

While we were up at the mine, I was energetically receiving download after download. I received an energetic upgrade to my system. I guess you can compare it to an upgrade to your computer software. Things I no longer needed were moved out while simultaneously new upgrades were brought in.

At the time, I had absolutely no idea what this meant.

The second thing Sandy told me was that when I was at the opening of the mine, the funny grumbling sound was a mountain lion living in the cave.

Whoa!

It wasn't until a few years ago that I dissected this experience. There is so much to unpack from it.

The Mountain Lion is the catalyst. In Shamanic practices, you are presented with a power animal who helps you on your soul's journey. They assist you as a guide, and in this case, a fierce protector. Over time, you can embody aspects of these glorious helpers. A Mountain Lion represents several things, but the most important to me during this time was Protection. It was specifically protection of the self, as I was beginning to redefine who I was.

An additional aspect the Mountain Lion exhibits is Adaptability and Agility. Being able to respond to this fundamental personal change was an integral part of my healing process. The gift of being sure-footed on my path to wholeness was a welcomed attribute. It also allowed me to have the ability to move through life with the beauty and grace of the Mountain Lion.

Another point of observation is demonstrated with the migraine. It represents the mental mind and its ability to not let go. Before arriving at the mountain, I was in an extremely overwhelmed state, trying to process multiple devastating layers of loss. I had an inability to define who I was. My identity and core beliefs about myself were systematically shattered through life events, one right after the other. With the mention of the multiple downloads from

The Mountain Lion's Grumble

nature, I was able to begin to deepen my spiritual practices. I gave myself permission to move through this expansion. I began to release the old thoughts patterns and beliefs that no longer aligned with me, allowing new ones to begin to create a foundation for my inner world.

There is so much symbolism in this allegory: the trail of dust, the breaking of the rocks, the protection, the dry bed stream, the opening of the mine, the mountain lion, the energetic downloads. All these things come together and create a beautiful analogy of a wounded hero's journey. All these glorious pieces are part of an awakening process.

Up until my trip out West, I had been on a path to healing. I choose to believe that the grumble of the mountain lion represents the start of my awakening process. I began to awaken to new ideas, new beliefs, and new thought patterns. I was awakening to new possibilities. It will always be an ongoing process. May your path to awakening bring you to new heights and levels of awareness each and every day!

Activities:

Are there specific animals that people continuously give you as gifts? Do people consistently comment about a specific animal to you? For example, "Whenever I see a butterfly, I think of you"?

Do you see multiple images of the same animal on your social media?

Look at the attributes of a power animal and see how it may align in your life. Consider how it appeared in your life and the lessons it offers.

Call on Mountain Lion help you:

- Move forward with faith and courage
- Boosting your confidence
- Need decisiveness, determination, and perseverance
- Maintaining your dignity and self-respect
- Achieving and pursuing your goals
- Clear and purposeful intention
- Leadership
- Patience when wanting more
- Persistence in getting what you want
- Claiming and owning your power
- Strong presence
- Overcoming procrastination
- Acting with resolve
- Need for solitude

Dawn Hamilton

Dawn Hamilton stands as a highly accomplished practitioner with a rich tapestry of certifications, including being a certified Akashic Record Healer Practitioner, Reiki Master (specializing in Angelic Reiki, 5 Element Dragon Fire Reiki, Holy Fire Reiki, and Usui Reiki), and holding additional expertise as a certified Crystalline Soul Healing ® practitioner and Light Language Healer.

With her holistic approach, Dawn skillfully navigates the intricacies of energy healing, bringing forth profound transformation. Guiding clients through the exploration of the Akashic Records, she uncovers hidden blocks and obstacles, offering insights that pave the way for deep personal and spiritual growth. Dawn's mastery of various Reiki modalities enhances her ability to channel universal life force energy, promoting balance on physical, emotional, and spiritual planes.

Her unique fusion of energy healing techniques and empowerment strategies creates a sacred space for clients to overcome challenges, empowering them to step into a life aligned with their true desires.

Dawn resides in Chicago, Illinois, with the love of her life Darryl, and their big dog Bo.

Email: Infinite.Illuminations8@gmail.com

Facebook: https://www.facebook.com/profile.php?id=100090897267003&mibextid=ZbWKwL

FOUR

From Trauma to Trust

Sara Talia Giza

Before I knew my last name, I knew the police. Before I knew laughter, I knew tears. Before I knew the sun, I saw the rain. It was raining that night. My sisters and I crawled into the back of my aunt's red van. *Where are we going? The darkness is out, surely, I must be dreaming for not long ago we three girls were put to bed.*

"Everything is going to be okay, girls," my grandma assured us from the passenger seat. I watched the drops fall onto the windshield. The wipers worked feverishly. There was no point. The water just ran off on its own, as if it, too, did not wish to exist.

Parked out front of a 7-Eleven convenience store, we waited patiently for the lady on the pay phone. Who is she talking to? My aunt made no sense, standing there in the rain on a phone. "As soon as your aunt Jan gets off the phone, we'll be going back to get your mom," Grandma said calmly. Jan hopped into the van, soaking from head to toe. "They're on the way," she whispered to my grandma as if we were not there at all. Yes, spare the children. They'll learn the words soon enough.

We were in motion, yet moving so slowly. Jan passed cautiously by our house. "They're not there yet," my aunt said. "Better drive around the block," Grandma instructed. She drove for a while more, and I wondered if we would make it home at all. This time, as she crept along, she made the turn. Our driveway, long and wide, was full of other cars. They were white and black. There were lights. Blue and red.

I saw my father emerge from the house. He walked towards us. Just as he got close enough to the van that held us captive in safety, the men surrounding him pulled him in another direction. His hands were behind him as if his arms no longer worked. They bent him over, and he got into the white and black vehicle with the pretty flashing lights.

"Daddy!" I screamed, "Where are they taking my daddy?" I tried to get out of the van. I wanted to run to him. I wanted to hug him.

At that moment, my mother arrived with her soaked face and glazed eyes with a smile that still looked like a frown even when she thought she was pulling it off. "You can't go with Daddy," she said. "You stay with me now."

Struggling, my arms twisted, and I flailed, trying with all of my might to escape—to run to him.

"Sara, stop! You will stay with me now." She arranged herself in the back of the van and pulled me onto her lap. She sniffled in my ear as I cried on her chest. I was only two years old that night. It was the first time I saw my father get arrested for beating my mother and holding her hostage.

For years, I suffered from recurring nightmares from that night, from that first memory of life. I would always wake myself up from the crying. I would awake with tears rolling down my face, just like that two-year-old girl in the dream, so vivid were those images that haunted me on a regular basis until I was about sixteen. I was haunted by the girl who still believed in her father. At that age, I was not able to comprehend that he had done something bad. To little girls, fathers are superheroes who can do no wrong. But, in time, I learned.

In time, I learned about shifty eyes and the sounds of things shattering against the walls. In time, I learned how to take a beating. I learned that they will beat you until you cry loud enough and then beat you until you are silent. I guess it was my fault for never learning quite the right amount. I learned how to run down the hall and lock my little sister in her room.

"You lock this door, and you do not come out until I tell you to, until I come for you. You understand?" I learned how to run down the hall and call 911.

A variety of trauma was always on tap. We were from Flint, Michigan, a town in itself that has a never-ending stench of macro trauma for the residents as well as any person who hears stories about it. The proprietor of multiple systemic issues. We were a pretty traditional poor family. Three small children being raised by a single mother who often worked two jobs and was absent out of necessity, we lived for a time in government housing. Being surrounded by alcoholism, substance abusers, and drug dealers was the norm. We moved so many times that I can't remember the names of all of the schools I attended. After a while, I stopped trying to make friends. Soon enough, I'd be leaving anyway with my bag already packed full of the knowledge that I would not know stability.

Of all the things I learned from my childhood to adolescence, the one thing I did not was self-worth. In my life, I have endured every kind of abuse known to man—verbal, physical and that which does not deserve a name. No one protected me, and nobody, not once, stopped to ask me if I was okay. Of all that got swept under the rug, the greatest of these things was me.

As an adult, I have come to realize the power of words, to give the unspeakable a voice. You must own it, so it does not own you. My journey, long and complex, has often been a battle. I struggle every day, every single day, to rise above, to undo what has been done, to rewrite my story, to choose to love instead of hate. Self-worth is something I have had to teach myself, and many times, I failed.

I committed horrible acts of violence on myself. I went backwards and took the long way, always making it harder for myself. I let the wrong people in and kept the right ones out. I built so many walls; my fortress was strong. I thought I was keeping the bad away, but instead, I was keeping it all in. I had self-sabotage on lockdown. Mostly, I was foolish enough for a long time to make myself believe that what I had endured had no effect on me at all.

Even those closest to me do not know my whole story. I was made to be silent for so long that now that I am free, I move my lips to speak, but no words come out. I firmly believe that those who have experienced trauma and have been exposed to domestic, sexual, or emotional abuse need to be empowered to tell their story. Children should never be silenced. They should know that what they have experienced is a part of them, but it is not them. I can say with great certainty, had I been encouraged to express myself as a child, my life would have been very different.

Admittedly, my pre-teen years were filled with a smidge more angst than the usual lot. I couldn't seem to resist an argument with my mother, a debate, on just how fucked up everything was. In retrospect, I was brimming with rage. A pissed-off child is a child in pain. It is far easier to be mad than admit that we are hurting. Never having gotten much external validation, I caved inward to my introverted, hermit shell. I couldn't seem to relate to kids my age. Most of my memories are of me by myself. Sitting on the bed, listening to the radio. Alone. Meanwhile, the kids laughing outside could be heard through my window.

Although enrolled in Catholic Sunday School as a child to appease our family, my mother wasn't devout. With a childhood sadly worse than ours, she would often seek solace from a surrogate mother figure and mentor, named Betty. We knew that Betty would "read cards" to our mom and advise her, but we really didn't grasp the entirety of what that meant—only that our mom took it seriously and recorded their conversations. While visiting Betty's house, I often got a "feeling" that I was being watched when no one was physically there. It wasn't until decades later that I realized Betty was, in fact, a light worker and psychic, and that I, too, had a "gift."

Once I was in high school, it wasn't uncommon for me to skip school. I would wake up and head out, but hop on a city bus instead and spend the day roaming around town in Tucson, Arizona. Adults involved turned an eye due to my ability to maintain honor roll consistently and not be a "problem kid" for the teachers. As always, I found the most solace in silence and being alone. Frequenting used bookstores, I loved the smell and sight of books. Being surrounded by so much knowledge, knowing perfectly well that I could never learn all of it, I was still unwaveringly excited by what great treasure I might stumble upon. During this time, I gravitated to learning as much about the spiritual realm as possible. Along with my mom's mentor Betty, I had also heard that my Syrian great-grandmother, who immigrated to the United States, used to read tea leaves. I knew enough to know that I didn't know enough.

Books on Buddhism, Hinduism, the history of ancient Middle Eastern culture—I devoured them all, along with books on meditation and how to meet your spirit guides. Putting into practice what I had read, I asked the divine to meet my spirit guide. And, to my surprise, it delivered!

One night, during a meditative state that landed somewhere between the realms of awake and asleep, a face appeared to me so vividly. I asked directly, "Are you my spirit guide?"

The figure, which was male and with eyes that seemed to be the blue ocean itself, said "Yes." He had the kindest eyes I have ever seen. There was a peace in that moment that I had never experienced before. Immediately, I was in it. I not only embraced exploring and practicing my spiritual gifts but was in love with it. I learned different divination tools like tarot cards, held special rituals for the moon cycles, and began collecting stones and herbs: all of the tools needed to stay connected with the spiritual realm, but also with myself.

To my surprise, the more often I utilized them, my gifts seemed to grow. Always sensitive to energy, I would later become Clairsentient and a Reiki practitioner. It wasn't uncommon for me to catch a glimpse of a human figure out of the corner of my eye, only for the image to be gone as soon as I gave it my full attention. Spirits walk around us all the time!

Premonitions started to pop up. While still in high school, I had what seemed like a very random dream one night. While asleep, I dreamed that a male peer I had only known from a distance but felt a great pull towards walked into my sixth-period Sociology class and joined it. The next day at school, much to my shock, the exact same thing happened! He walked right into my class. The universe has a funny way of putting people who are important for our path next to us. Other premonitions came and went, yet I never stopped being surprised at how my intuition, with no facts of any kind, always seemed to be right. It's hard to believe in your gifts when you were never taught to believe in yourself.

Despite the wounding of my childhood, there were also gifts. Perhaps, the greatest of these was the development of my empathy. Empathy led to my career in social work. I never want anyone to have to suffer in silence. No one should have to feel alone. Prior to private practice, I worked for over a decade in nonprofits, including two different dual domestic violence/rape crisis centers as a Sexual Assault Victim Advocate. Unless you've been there, it's hard to understand the profoundness of being called in the middle of the night to race to a local hospital to be with a survivor who was just sexually assaulted. To hold their hand as they cry on your chest, during the Sexual Assault Forensic Exam. This is not a job that I would recommend to anyone. The vicarious trauma is so immense and, at times, the toll immeasurable. But someone has to do it. I am someone. I can and will do it.

There is great pain in those moments, but also great beauty—their willingness to trust me so openly with that level of vulnerability. This is the duality present all throughout our lives. I wouldn't be so great at what I do if I didn't know what it's like to be on the other side. We have a choice to act out of kindness or hate. We get to choose to repeat cycles or break them. Being able to balance both darkness and light is the greatest test we will take while here in these bodies.

There were times when I turned my back on the divine—not out of disdain or disbelief, but out of everyday distraction and responsibility. I did not have a perfect beginning. I have no illusions that any portion of my life will be perfect. But what I do trust is this: I am always perfectly protected and guided by the divine. And so are you!

Reclaiming the Spiral

Looking at a labyrinth can be lovely, but it's no fun when one lives inside of your head. When we experience trauma or encounter upsetting experiences along our journey, it is common to try to make sense of it by looking for the cause. Often, the first finger we point is directly at ourselves.

If I was just better…
  If only I did (fill in the blank)…
  I should've done x, instead of y or z and this wouldn't have happened…
  They wouldn't have _____, unless I deserved it…

We seek out a cause for the faulty sense of control it gives us. If we knew why something happened, we could prevent it from happening again—or so we think. Our need to connect the dots only does more damage, as it lowers our self-esteem and leads to spiraling into shame that we somehow actively contributed to those painful moments or caused them entirely. The blame only ever belongs to the perpetrator.

This is your spiral. Start at the center and walk yourself out of any self-blame or feelings of shame, by writing out the truth kindly to yourself. Make a return visit to read your statement, any time you start to feel yourself slipping back, about to pick up what is not yours to carry.

"Don't turn your head. Keep looking at the bandaged place. That's where the light enters you."
~Rumi, Persian Poet and Mystic (d. 1273)

Journal Prompt

In ancient Greek Mythology and Astrology, Chiron was a Centaur. The half-human-half-horse was renowned for his ability to transmute the suffering and pain of others. Yet, once wounded, he was not able to heal himself, thus giving birth to the archetype of the "wounded healer." Even famed psychotherapist Carl Jung explored this concept. In 1957, he posited in "Fundamental Questions of Psychotherapy" that the best training for a doctor may, in fact, be having a disease.

What gifts and knowledge have you received from the trials and tribulations of your own life?

From Trauma to Trust

Sara Talia Giza

Sara Talia Giza, MSW, LSWAIC, is a queer social worker, award-winning freelance writer, and healing initiator. With expertise in trauma, she has helped countless teens and adults overcome their unique challenges and start down the pathway to healing through her practice. She has served on the state of Kentucky's human trafficking task force and has a certification from the University of Pennsylvania on violence and abuse prevention.

As a writer, Sara was the senior editor for *Embrace Magazine*, Central Florida's first publication dedicated to the LGBTQ+ population. Most recently, her work has appeared in the *Willamette Week* and *Vancouver Family Magazine*. As a clairsentient, lightworker, and Reiki practitioner, she is passionate about highlighting the good in this world and increasing it. She draws upon the nurturing and strength found within nature to sustain her.

Connect with her via Email at saragiza@yahoo.com, her website https://www.psychologytoday.com/us/therapists/sara-giza-vancouver-wa/1019075 or on Instagram @searingsara

FIVE

Caverna

Dawn Sullivan

I had been telling myself since I turned 45 that the next half of my life would be the best half; 2023 was the year I turned 50. This was my year! A brisk plunge in the Atlantic on January 1st was the beginning—Happy New Year to me!

This was also the year I began working with my inner child, really engaging with her, having dialogues with her, and inviting in playfulness and curiosity. Choosing to heal my inner child was a turning point, shifting the way I approached *everything*.

It was really as I found my inner child that I simultaneously chose to become intentional about where I spent my time and energy. Turning 50 meant picking certain themes in my life that would aid in healing old parts of me–the wounded self–so that I could continue stepping into the best possible version of myself. This new energy of play brought about more tools to help work with my wounds and begin my journey into recovery from a binge eating disorder. I created endless art journals and a bucket list of adventures. Riding a horse, a boudoir photo shoot and visiting an ashram were a few of them.

Reflecting back on a session with my art therapist, I also knew that beginning my manuscript would be on the list. "Dawn, What would you do with the time that you are not compulsively eating?" The answer was already there and had been for years. On the first day of spring, I began writing the manuscript for my memoir.

During the summer months, I worked on self-compassion and self-acceptance of my physical body, exactly as it was and is. I began my yoga practice and gently pushed myself through limitations. I learned and continue to learn to love every single part. I began to get comfortable taking photos of myself. On the last day of summer, I celebrated by going to the ocean and taking pictures of myself in my swimsuit. It was much warmer than in January, but just as invigorating. I felt alive and free!

Fall was all about working with my shadow self: really diving deep into my recovery and unpacking my shit while deepening my self-discovery. With the energy of the new moon on Friday, October 13th, I took a powerful part of myself back with my boudoir session. The set included a casket and silver wings. In a sense, I had died and come back to life freer than ever.

During the winter months, I chose to nourish myself from within and deepen my spirituality. This is how I landed at the yoga ashram during the Solstice weekend. There was no cellular service, everything was solar-powered, and there were minimal people around. It was just what I was yearning and craving, despite the darkness and frigid temps.

Prior to this sacred pilgrimage, I was having dreams of being in a cave or womb space. After analyzing these dreams, it all made sense: the darkest places are where seeds are planted, things begin to grow, come to life, and ideas are born.

I kept a very open mind about what I would experience. I was immersed in a culture where you shred the ego. I was there to experience "something" and release vanity.

Uma welcomed me warmly and showed me to my cabin. There were skylights over my bed, and because it was in northern Maine, away from light pollution, I was thrilled about seeing the stars that night. I settled in and waited with anticipation for the weekend to begin.

That evening after eating a delicious vegan meal with the

company of others, I needed a reprieve with my solitude to prepare for the evening's meditation ceremony.

I stepped out of the main house and headed to my cabin. There was a canopy of stars over my head. The darkness was almost frightening, but the sound of the babbling brook nearby brought me comfort.

The ramblings of my nine-year-old self crept in. She shouted, "I'M SCARED! I'M COLD!"

I comforted her.

She then asked, "What is my place here? What is my place in this world?"

I acknowledged her fear, *our* fear, and trekked on into the cold, dark night to my weekend of unknowns. With my headlamp illuminating only a few steps in front of me, it was as if I were The Hermit in the tarot deck. It was a sign of that card's message: the answers to my soul-searching would come from within when they needed to.

That evening's ceremony began with a lecture that nourished my soul. We chanted and then transitioned into an hour-long meditation. I sat cross-legged like the others for most of it. Despite my ego's comparative inner dialogue, I honored my body's cues and shifted as I needed to.

Saturday's agenda included several rituals, light refreshments, meeting the gurus, dancing, and a sauna session.

Trekking up the mountain for a meditative walk was the start of the day. I was adorned in my harem pants, hiking stick in tow. At the top, we each struck a huge gong that echoed through the misty mountaintop. Every cell of my being came alive with each ripple of the "BONG-SHHH" sound.

The yogi led us back down to pray. A fire was lit, oil and wood were placed, and the warmth was welcoming us in. We chanted, and our guide told us the pit symbolized a portal of the divine feminine. Was this the womb space that I had been envisioning?

I was so caught up in it, the music, the conch shells, the chanting, the fire, the incense—it was all so potent, magical, and spiritually intoxicating. One by one, folks went up to the center to contribute to the fire with oil and kindling and to bow in reverence for this Divine Spirit.

The photographer there began clickin' away for the ashram's media page. I quickly reminded myself why I was there: to let go of vanity and be my "self." The portal called me in. I dipped the wood into the oil and dropped it into the burning pit. I bowed in reverence, staying there for what seemed to be forever. I asked the Divine for massive healing.

I lifted my eyes to the Shiva as the yogi anointed my forehead with the ash and oil. Her dark brown eyes met mine. It felt like the fire within her had further ignited the fire within me.

After the ceremony, it was refreshment time, and while I was excited to taste a vegan dessert, I began to feel terribly ill. A migraine was approaching fast—pain behind my left eye and a feeling like I was going to vomit. I let Uma know that I had to sneak away as I wasn't feeling well. As soon as I walked into my cabin, I began to vomit. Vehemently.

There was no plumbing in the ashram, so I couldn't flush away the smell with my pain. Instead, I covered it up with peat moss and crept up to my room to fall asleep.

I awakened in the darkness—no light, no sound. It was the perfect environment to recover from a migraine, except it was cold. I couldn't exactly call up to the main house and ask someone to light a fire, so I pulled all the blankets over me and curled into the fetal position to keep warm.

It was as if my highest self knew my inner child's needs without words because miraculously, one of the guides showed up to light a fire and brought a bowl of turmeric rice and salad.

As I recovered, I read the Tao De Ching for the third time in my life. I read poetry by the great poet Rumi. I journaled and pulled some tarot cards. I did this for hours while the others continued in the retreat activities. I was so caught up, enraptured even, as I watched shooting stars through the skylight. I spoke with a sliver of the moon, and Ursa Major blinked answers like I had never seen her before. Visions of Quan Yin, Buddha, Jesus, and the apostles encircled my mind. I prayed in reverence for these deities. I was so thankful for this that I blissed out in meditation and then fell into a deep slumber.

Early Sunday morning, not wanting to awaken anyone, I gathered my belongings and drove home. The retreat itself was still on for most of the day, but I was eager to be in my own environment, my own room. I felt like that "something" that I went to the ashram to experience had already happened. I just couldn't put it into words—*yet*.

Driving along, it came to me that the incense was the cause of my migraine, but I also knew that I cleared something important from within. My inner dialogue with my 9-year-old self began again. She was mad that she didn't get dessert. Not wanting to make her feel punished by this, I drove to my old neighborhood to visit this old pine tree I used to climb. I got out of my car and put my hands on the tree, and then I hugged it. I snapped a pic. Same ole' tree, just bigger. We were both different now. I shuffled back into my car and pondered when and why I had replaced adventure with fear.

Walking into my home and finding a huge canvas waiting for me, I felt inspired to create. I pulled out my paints, magazines, and other supplies and began making the largest mixed-media piece I've ever created. I trusted my "calling" on the colors and images. Buddha, Jesus, and a photo of myself at 18 were among the many. This process felt like her (my 18-year-old self) healing.

With each stroke of the brush, limiting beliefs of insecurity about her body, her identity, feeling ugly, and the discomfort of being in her own skin all fell away. Playing, creating, releasing tears, and dancing with reckless abandon was so invigorating. At this moment, in this room, a new realization came; I had stopped actively creating when I was 18 years old. As a teenager, I would sit in my room for hours listening to music while making collages. My aunt Vicky, whom I had been living with since I was 14, had always encouraged my creativity and sense of play. She once told me that living in her house meant that I was safe to come out of my hiding place.

A few days later, during the actual winter solstice, most of

Maine lost power. I welcomed this since I had just returned from not having power at the ashram. Candles lit and a journal in hand, I did a visualization meditation at my kitchen table. I found myself in a field, wearing a long, flowing white dress. The wind was gently stirring, and my hair was tossing about in the breeze. I walked toward the end of the field, where there was a darkening, a mound of forest debris. As I got closer, I realized it was a small cave. I felt a presence.

Inching closer to this cave, I saw a creature: a very stiff, dark, and hairy beast-like thing. I approached it and asked it to come out to see me. I could see its hesitation, so I stretched out my hand. It didn't want to take my hand. I felt this immense loneliness coming from it. It had been abandoned. It felt alone and forgotten about, unseen, unheard–like it didn't matter.

I moved in closer and reached my other hand out, pulling the beast in for a gentle, tender hug. I said the words, "I love you." I jolted back to reality with the clicking sound of the fridge and flashing lights among my candles. This quickening came with the beast's name: Caverna, the Portuguese word for cave.

I honored the flow and grabbed my journal to unpack these feelings and emotions. Caverna is my wounded inner child/children. Unseen, unheard, un-belonging, and purposeless. To stay safe as a child, I hid and spoke very little. Instead of speaking the words I needed to speak, I stuffed them down with food while I hid. These behaviors served a purpose at one time, but I no longer needed them.

Within the safety of my journal, I was able to see a pattern of my whole self. The realization that within each room, as a child and adult, I was free to explore, discover, and express. It was enlightening to work with this juxtaposition of my inner child and highest self. They were one and the same: the child, unseen and unheard, but safe within the womb of the highest self.

What my inner children see as hiding was not hiding at all. It was a necessary means for this empathic soul to come away from a world that can be harsh and hurtful. I needed these moments of freedom and safety. Caverna, my shadow self, saw the solitude as isolation and being unseen, the silence as being unheard. She misunderstood the solitude time as *powerless*, not **powerful**. When I am caught up in my room, I forget the world for a while, Caverna saw this as being forgotten *about*. A mother may not see or hear her baby in her womb space; she feels the presence. She provides safety and protection from within for growth. The infant takes up space and then emerges.

Virginia Woolf called it *A Room of One's Own*. For me, those walls were symbolic of "A Womb of One's Own."

The last bits of wisdom came about as I continued writing in my journal: I flashed back to my tree. Near the top, there was a limb that I sat on and sometimes rocked with excitement. With this rocking came a crack, and we both crashed. Something that supported me hurt me. Love was replaced with fear.

Little Dawn took that broken limb from the tree and made a place to hide. As they grew together with each season, every storm, and each limb that fell, the further in she went—until one day—it became crystal clear that my purpose is to alchemize darkness into light.

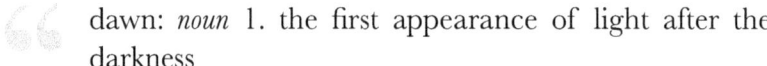

dawn: *noun* 1. the first appearance of light after the darkness

When one of us heals, it creates a ripple effect out into the world so that we can all heal. If we can become intentional about our healing, actively participate, and do the challenging work, however it looks to each of us, we can emerge out of the darkness into the birthright of our whole self.

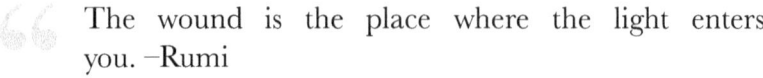

The wound is the place where the light enters you. –Rumi

1. By using the following tarot themes, how can you empower yourself to work *with* the flow of the seasons?

The Year: *X. Wheel of Fortune: Life Cycles, Turning Point, Change*

Create a list of adventures you would like to do for the year, the month, the week, the day.

Spring: *III. The Empress: Creativity, Nature, Beauty.*

What do you want to create? Is there a place in nature you want to visit?

Summer: *XIX. The Sun: Positivity, Play, Vitality*

Where in your life can you bring in play? Write a gratitude list!

Autumn: *XIII. Death: Transformation, Change, Endings*

What can you let go of? What is no longer serving your highest self?

Winter: *XVII. The Star: Hope, Purpose, Renewal*

Recognize a dark time in your life, how has this given you a sense of hope? What is your purpose?

2. Take a walk in nature and find a place that you consider unsightly. Sit with it for a moment. Take a few deep breaths, if that feels supportive. Get curious about how this part of the forest is beneficial to the rest of the forest. Do you see any hidden gems? Is there any wisdom that it has to share? Draw your answers here. Use stick figures if you like. Use crayons, paints or anything you have on hand. Process art has so much to offer us if we are open to it. Trust yourself! Play! Allow what comes up for you and journal with it.

3. Create your own cave. In the woods, with bed sheets or whatever you have!

Dawn Sullivan

Dawn Sullivan is sweet like sugar but accepts her shadow side; she can be a little salty if needed! She is awkwardly adorable and wants everyone to succeed. While this is her first published work, her art is featured in Tookie Bright's *Insight and Aracana*. Dawn is a tarot reader for self-discovery and growth with the *9 Lives Tarot*. She lives in Central Maine and loves being out in nature.

Her new YouTube channel is SoulPlay, where you can find healing and recovery through art and play. Dawn's memoir, *A Life of Pages*, is planned to be released in Spring of 2025. This is also the year that she will add skydiving to her adventure list!

Links linktr.ee/dawn.sullivan

SIX

Weaving Magic in the Shadows to Create Harmony Between Light and Dark

Michelle Hamady

LIGHTS OUT

My childhood was a wild mix of experiences. Between the abuses, the molestations, the potential abductions, deep depression, suicide attempts, and running away from home–how could I love my childhood? It doesn't make sense that I would, but I do because of the magic that also surrounded me.

My memories hold my endless love and fascination with nature and animals and all the joy of unleashing my curiosity to explore the world around me. Within these memories, all my pain was also held.

That was the paradox of my life.

It wasn't until many years later when I eventually learned how to stop fearing the dark, that I learned to see all the magic that was obscured.

DON'T BE AFRAID OF THE DARK

Deep down within, there's a brave inner child who has been trying to hold it all together herself the best she could, the only way she knew how. Early on, she learned that to be safe, she was the only one who could protect her. She learned to stay hidden in the shadows. That's where she felt safest.

She was never afraid of the dark, because she was already there.

WELCOME TO MY WORLD

We live in a world of duality between the constant swinging pendulum from black to white, light to dark, pain to pleasure, joy to sorrow. Navigating the spaces in between can sometimes create a level of anxiety. The uncertainty that comes from stepping into the unknown can stop you in your tracks, or it can give birth to the magic and mystery that come from its exploration. The duality within the shadows holds the magic of shadow alchemy.

This is where I feel the most comfortable, not because I'm afraid of the dark or because I love the light, but because the shadows are where I find my power.

I was born into that in-between space. As the first-born child to a mixed-race couple, I entered into my world already divided. On top of that, my soul decided my birthplace would be Seoul, within the divided country of Korea. (My soul sure does have a sense of humor!) And if that wasn't enough, within months of my birth, my dad's next military assignment meant we were relocating to the United States.

Surrounded by a swirling sea of conflicting energies rooted in divisiveness, I had no stable foundation or roots to feel safely anchored. I longed for a sense of belonging. Welcome to my world–and this was just the beginning.

MAGIC WAITS IN THE SHADOWS

My early childhood memories are rooted in, and surrounded by darkness and shadows–literally. I remember my kindergarten class was in the basement of a building aptly named the Little Red Schoolhouse. Oh, the simplicity of such a name in a complex period of my life! In hindsight, I now see how this foreshadowed–no pun intended there–much of my life.

On my very first day of school, I remember entering the building and being immediately escorted, along with other students, up a flight of stairs to the top floor. The entire area seemed well-lit from the bright sunlight filtering in through all the classroom windows. I had been assigned to Room 1, which was located to the right. My feelings of excitement and first-day jitters were soon replaced with a sense of chaos and confusion as the staff realized that the classroom was over capacity.

Several students were quickly reassigned and sent to other rooms. I was guided back down the flight of stairs to the main entryway once again, and then down another set of steps to the basement. My new room assignment was Room 5. It was the last room and happened to be in the basement. (Oh, the metaphors and symbolism here!)

As I reflect on this moment, I can't help but acknowledge how this basement classroom symbolized my childhood perfectly. In contrast to the bright open room I had just left, this one had a softer, diffused light. It felt isolating yet strangely cozy. I felt safe enough to have fun and even be mischievous. Perhaps this was setting the stage for my training ground, where I would begin to learn to find comfort in the shadows.

In what now seems like a flip of a switch, the transition between kindergarten classrooms mirrored the shift in my young life at that time, as darkness began to take hold in other areas at home. Confusion became a prevailing energy in my life as I struggled to find freedom in the shadows while beginning to fear the light. Feeling tucked away in this dimly lit classroom, this quickly became one of my safe havens.

IN THE DARK, LIES THE TREASURES

In the basement of my mind are the stored memories of darkness no young child should ever have to experience.

By the time I was 5, I had experienced sexual abuse from two different men. The first was a stranger to me, but someone my dad trusted. He handed me over to be momentarily watched, thinking I would be safe and protected. I wasn't.

The other was my dad. Once again, the person who was supposed to protect me became my abuser. Violent outbursts and rage would erupt from the nurturing father I had trusted and looked up to. It's as if overnight, in the blink of an eye, the father I adored, who also had adored me, no longer seemed to exist. Was it something I did?

Seeking protection or comfort from my mom was never an option either. She was inconvenienced and embarrassed by my fears and emotions and therefore dealt with it by punishing and shaming me for showing any signs of them. Both of my parents were trapped in their own pain, unable to provide for my needs.

Betrayed by a father with no one to turn to, I found my safety outside the walls of my home. For many, home is normally considered to be a safe space. For me, it was anywhere else but home. I craved my safe spaces at school and outside in nature as much as possible. This is where I could find clarity because I wasn't swimming in the pain of others, drowning in a muddy mess of emotions, and getting lost in the foggy confusion. If I was deeply connected and rooted to my inner knowing, I had the clarity of knowing what I needed, and who I was. With that, I knew I was always safe.

My sensitivity and inquisitive nature were considered problems. I learned early on, according to the adults in my life, that I was the problem; I took this belief into myself, and it festered and morphed to become my new identity. This idea continued to grow into a bigger belief that being seen was not a good thing.

In my world, the darkness held the pain, but it was the light where it was created. I believed being seen was dangerous because that's where the abuse happened, and the attacks would take place. Even though nothing bad happened in the dark, that's where the pain was held. The light held my fear. I stayed in the shadows to avoid both until I learned how to safely dive into the dark, not get lost, to feel safe to be seen in the light and shine my light. The shadows gave me the protection I needed.

It was an endless loop of pain that created more pain. Invisibility became my shield, and I remained out of sight as much as possible.

I learned to stay in the shadows, that's where it was the safest. A few years passed, and during my 4th grade, my dad died. Shortly afterward, I spiraled down into the depths of darkness I didn't think I'd ever make it out of. I was overwhelmed by depression, followed by suicide attempts and self-mutilation. Somehow, I managed to survive, and at the age of 14, I ran away from home.

OUT OF THE DARKNESS

Before I left home, the crucial turning point came around the age of 11 or 12.

I was leaving the local library one day after spending a few hours there. The library was another one of my favorite spots and was in the center of town a couple miles from my home. The books fueled my curiosity in my quest for knowledge, which helped me make sense of my world and that helped me feel safe. I spent as much time there as I could.

This particular day, I noticed a figure behind me, and I recognized him. He was a man I had seen many times in passing, usually from the safety of my school bus. He was always alone and could be seen yelling, fighting, boxing, and cussing out imaginary opponents.

He was quite a distance away, so I felt reassured and continued my walk. If there was some distance between us, I felt safe. Of course, with his stride and his speed, it didn't take long for him to begin gaining on me. Suddenly, he caught up to me.

I had stopped at the main intersection of my small town. The familiar sight of the Little Red Schoolhouse was on the corner diagonally from where I stood. To my right was the corner opposite the schoolhouse, where there was a tiny cemetery lot and an old white church with a buckling foundation.

Before I had time to react to the full realization that he had caught up to me, I remember hearing his words commanding me, "You're going to go where I tell you to go!"

In that split second, panic and fear quickly turned into defiance!

How dare he tell ME what to do! And the words shot out of my mouth, "Oh no, I'm not!" as I began to make a beeline to the center of the intersection.

Talk about a pattern interrupt! The look on his face was a mix of shock and panic as he hurried away. He looked at me as if I was the crazy one while quickly trying to distance himself from me, not wanting any attention to be drawn his way.

At that moment, the adrenaline rush kicked in full gear, and I felt so empowered! This stranger gave me the priceless gift of realizing I could defend myself in a way I could never defend myself at home. At home, I had no choice but to receive what I was subjected to, although it went against every fiber of my being. I was forced to be the obedient little girl. Outdoors, I had the power to say no and protect myself. I discovered there is safety in the light, and being visible can be a powerful thing.

My new identity was taking shape. A spark had ignited, and something was coming alive in me again.

During the time after that, I had built up enough courage to leave home. That's when, at 14 years old, I led myself out of the darkness, but I had to go into it to get through it. And so, I did. Out the window to my freedom. In the middle of the night.

The darkness held my power, and in the shadows, I was reclaiming it.

INTO THE LIGHT

Over the years, there were times when I felt stuck in the in-between space, fearing the darkness would pull me in: fearing I would be unable to find my way back out. That was until I learned to dive for the light: for my light. To discover and reclaim my gifts that were long-buried and deeply hidden.

Like magicians who work their magic through the shadows, I, too, worked my way through the shadows to transform my pain into gifts.

You can spend time avoiding the dark, but once you embrace it, you find those treasures.

That's what I did. I became more comfortable each time, diving deeper and deeper, feeling more comfortable until the shadows became my new comfort zone. The familiar. The known. And that's when it shifted again. I realized the fear of the dark no longer had power over me. It was the light I still feared because I still held the old memories and beliefs that that's where the danger always takes place.

Fortunately, there comes a time when you realize there's so much healing that can occur when you accept that your light matters—when you realize you must show up in the light to help find others and lead the way out.

You become aware of how you've cultivated the necessary strength. You have the courage. You know the magic of alchemy and how powerful the process is. Then, you realize how important it is to share this with others.

This is Shadow Alchemy: facing the fears, embracing the light, playing in the spaces in between, and dancing in the shadows to weave the healing threads between light and dark that transform painful lessons into valuable gifts.

You get to collect the treasures to share with others.

IT'S TIME TO SHINE!

With each chapter of my life I heal and transform, I'm able to continue to help my inner child in her healing by empowering her with a new story.

I get to share the story with her of how she didn't hide; instead, she chose to bravely tap into her inner strength to do what was necessary to survive. She's reminded of the times she learned to skillfully navigate around danger. I help her see how she courageously protected her preciousness as I explain to her the story of an oyster. There's a hard shell surrounding a soft, vulnerable inside, and if an irritating grain of sand finds its way inside, a pearl is formed. This pearl has been safely forming for many years—a perfect pearl in all its treasured magnificence.

Then most importantly, I tell her how loved she is, how valued she's always been.

And now, the inner child realizes she is the pearl—and it's finally safe for her to come out and shine.

YOU ARE ALSO THE PEARL, AND IT'S YOUR TIME TO SHINE

In this world of duality, there will always be shadows and spaces between the light and dark. Power comes from the choice you make—what do you choose to do with the shadows? Do you freeze with fear and avoid the unknown, or do you engage the mystery and explore it?

I encourage you to dive into the unknown and dive deep for the light.

It's never too late to rewrite your story as you heal and move forward. May this be the first page of your new story!

WELCOME TO YOUR NEW STORY

First, before we begin, there's something you need to know.

Know that you are enough. In this moment. In every moment.

Take a deep breath and breathe in these words: I AM ENOUGH. As you slowly exhale, feel that, remember it.

You may have been through a life that also didn't make sense, and somehow you made it. You never gave up and didn't let things stand in the way. Your courageous resilience has made you who you are, and your tenacity has gotten you here. Today, you're here with an open heart, full of compassion. You've maintained your invaluable sensitive nature and never stopped caring deeply—and that doesn't seem to make sense either.

But it does!

You have a story to tell, and it makes complete sense.

So, grab your favorite journal and have a pen or pencil ready. Light a candle if you'd like. Let's dive in.

There are four parts to this activity section.

PART 1 – THE STARTING POINT IS ALWAYS YOU

Start by being centered and grounded in the present moment by taking a deep breath in. As you do, bring your awareness back to you and the space you're currently in. Hold that breath for a count of four. As you slowly exhale, release all those energies that are not yours and let go of any tension in your body. Close your eyes and tune into your body. Check in and sense, feel, or notice how you're feeling emotionally, mentally, and physically. Do this without judgment, just noticing. Next, tune into your immediate surroundings. What do you feel, sense, or notice? Can you sense the difference between your inner world and the external world?

Open your eyes and journal what came up for you. This is a great check-in exercise to do throughout the day. When you're able to stay centered and anchored in who you are, this will help support you from feeling lost.

PART 2 – HONOR WHO YOU ARE

Let's take a look at the parts that make you who you are.

You probably have many painful wounds you've been carrying around. Don't worry, we're not going to dig into your pain and wounds. That's not pleasant for anyone. Instead, we'll look at the themes around them. Do you have painful memories/beliefs associated with being too sensitive? Did you care too deeply when no one else did? Did you feel like you were too different and didn't belong? Worried about not being enough? Worried about doing the wrong thing?

This list can be many layers deep so we're not touching on all of them.

I'm sure you have many amazing traits–let's acknowledge those, too! Which ones are you most proud of? Some possibilities could be courage and curiosity to look for ways to keep going. Resilience and resourcefulness in always finding a way? Determination, tenacity, and commitment to self while refusing to give up? Never compromising your truth?

Just like your wounds, the list of your amazing traits can also be endless, and they all contribute to your unique brilliance.

Journal what memories came up for you as you reflected on these fragments of Light and Dark within you. When we look at these memories through the lens of love, we get to shine a light on many wounds that are ready to be seen and released. We give these wounds and ourselves a chance to be seen, acknowledged, and healed in the process.

PART 3 – THE SPACE IN BETWEEN WHERE MAGIC CAN HAPPEN

Now, we'll explore your current relationship with shadows.

Stepping into shadows can evoke a sense of fear of the unknown and discomfort in the uncertainty. Sometimes staying hidden in the shadows can provide a sense of safety, and it becomes a comfort zone. Which option do you tend to favor?

Either option can leave you feeling lost, disoriented, and afraid to go in one direction or another, becoming frozen in the shadows. The fear and uncertainty prevent you from taking the next step. However, to be truly empowered is to use the shadows for the "shadow work"–the work of weaving the Dark and Light and engaging in the mystery of it. In this exploration is where the magic is. This is where we find our power again, reclaiming the gifts from the dark to shine them in the light.

Journal on your relationship with shadows. Where can you reclaim your power? The safety you sought through invisibility becomes your real safety in visibility. When you take away the power of invisibility, you have the power in visibility.

PART 4 – WEAVING YOUR NEW STORY

There's a reason why you care deeply and have a huge compassionate heart– to be able to hold these memories and see them through your heart's lens, release the pain with love, and heal yourself back to wholeness.

You survived with a lifetime of stories that are evidence of how incredible you are! As you dance through the shadows, stepping into

Weaving Magic in the Shadows to Create Harmony Between Light and ...

the Dark and the Light, it's time to weave your new story and start your new chapter.

Reflect on your courageous life and think back to a pivotal moment that anchored in more of who you are. Maybe it was an act of bravery for finally taking a stand for yourself. Maybe it was compassion for saving a baby bird when no one else cared. Maybe it was speaking up for someone else who was voiceless. These are just some examples of the endless possibilities as unique as you are.

Can you now see the gift within that pivotal moment? What was it?

When you illuminate those dark areas, you shine a little brighter.

Now, it's time to rewrite your story.

In your journal, write your new story, and be sure to read it back aloud when you're done. You'll see how empowering it is and how your story makes perfect sense now.

I'll even venture to say you are more than enough, and you are probably freaking amazing! You have a story to share. Are you ready to step out of the shadows and shine your light? I hope you are. It's time. The world is ready for you.

Michelle Hamady

Michelle is a Creative Possibilities Alchemist and Transformation Coach, an International Best-Selling Author, and has an M.A. in Transpersonal Studies, with a specialization in Transformative Visual Arts through Atlantic University, Virginia Beach. She is passionate about helping others experience their inner power so that they remember their beauty, strength, and creative potential. She offers an innovative transformational process to guide individuals through their own self-discovery and healing journey to reveal just how amazing they truly are.

As a lifelong learner fueled by curiosity, she has discovered that life's aha moments are abundant, and the possibilities are endless in the self-development journey. Michelle is also a Reiki Master/Teacher in Usui Reiki Ryoho and 5 Element Dragon Fire Reiki, as well as a Certified Akashic Records Healer Practitioner.

Michelle has traveled to many energetic vortexes, such as the pyramids and temples of Egypt, Petra in Jordan, the Patagonia region in Chile, Morocco, Easter Island, the Canary Islands, and Sedona. Her spiritual journeys have instilled the courage necessary to navigate a chaotic corporate world while remaining soul-centered. She recently retired after 25 successful years in the corporate world to focus her time on helping others experience their own heart expansion through creative expression.

She believes we're all here to make our unique contribution to the world. By healing one heart and soul at a time, each of us can make an impact that will be felt in the world around us.

Website: https://michellehamady.com/
Facebook: https://www.facebook.com/michelle.hamady/
Linktree: https://linktr.ee/michellehamady

SEVEN

The Journey to Wholeness

Penny Sisley

"You were raised without a core of love, and since you have never had it, you don't know it's missing," Rajada said in our first mentoring session.

"How do you mean?" I asked, fed up with the idea of still not feeling whole.

"Your Mom wasn't raised with it either, so let's not look to blame anyone," he continued.

"But I've been reading and working on my self-awareness since I was 16 years old, I mean, when is it enough?" I said, noticing the resistance creeping up my spine.

"We'll get to that, for now, let's meditate and open your third eye."

The next day, I told my husband what Rajada said.

"That doesn't sound far from the truth," he replied. "You have always needed and looked on the outside of yourself for love and validation."

A scowl formed on my face.

Cautiously, he went on; "From the way I was raised, there is nothing on the outside that makes me less or changes my value up or down on the inside. Whatever I do doesn't change… me. Maybe what Raja said is why you people please to exhaustion?"

Husband is a brave man. My cheeks were searing hot, filled with blood. He was right.

A new beginning:
After three years and thousands of mantras, sweat, and that disruptive conversation, a whole new paradigm began to appear.

Aristotle said, "Knowing yourself is the beginning to all wisdom." That simple statement meant to me that after enough therapy, meditation, books, mentors and seminars, I would finally understand myself as a human and feel whole.

But, that's not what he meant.

Crack open any of your favorite teachings. You will begin to notice they are all talking about "your inner self," "your internal guidance," and your "inner knowing." I sensed they were not referring to knowledge or our brain; they were talking about the "I AM" and our connection to source energy inside of us, wisdom and love.

In the book, *One Truth, One Law: I AM, I CREATE*, by Erin Werley, Erin has a tangible conversation with a voice inside of her one day in the shower. She could tell it was not her own voice in her head she was talking to because it felt different in her body.

In UNTAMED, the literary masterpiece by Glennon Doyle, she explains how when she needs clarity, she lays down, does her best to clear her mind, and waits for a warmth to rise up in her system. At this point, she asks for guidance and always receives the best possible answer. Same with Erin.

For those who read the Bible, a verse in Psalms states: "I will instruct you and teach you in the way which you should go; I will counsel you with My eye upon you."

What are we?
Eckhart Tolle, a modern-day ascended master, refers in *The Power of Now* to this life energy within us as our Transcendent

Dimension of Consciousness. With the access point to this "other" dimension of ourselves being the now, he explains this is why the now is so important. The now is this very moment we are breathing in and breathing out, without the chaos of the past or future. Try it on.

In Michael Singer's *The Untethered Soul* books, we begin to unravel the possibility of us being energy in action rather than only having a solid physical state. With this ancient idea, we can learn to let go of the past and future and flow with the now. This allows the energy happening through us, this life energy Michael lovingly refers to as "She," to guide us into the most beautiful part of being alive. We become aligned and flow with our true nature - this moment.

Michael also explores who we are: so if you are a nurse, a mom, a sister and a wife, who are you if those things fall away? You get divorced, you retire, and friends or family pass. What are you then? And what about the athlete who can no longer compete due to a major injury, or the waitress who quits her job? What are they now?

We are not our relationships, and we are not what we do. I can say I'm Mexican or American, but what would I be if I lived in the same place 800 years ago when neither of those ideas existed? The only thing we can kind of claim is that we are an expression of energy in this moment, and only for the moment, then we are the next moment.

Esther Hicks, known for her ability to "channel" source energy referred to as Abraham, calls this inner guidance our inner entity or inner being, which is connected to the All, or source energy. The All is everything, physical and non-physical, past, present, future and in all dimensions, including our thoughts. We are source energy in a physical expression.

Tat tvam asi in Sanskrit means, "That thou art." "That" is everything. The All. We are the All.

When Jesus said, "Do unto others as you would have done unto yourself," he meant we are all one, so what you do to others, you are doing to yourself because you are the others. This is the beginning teaching of Unity Consciousness and the All. To understand Unity

Consciousness it helps to also understand Separation Consciousness.

TWIN FLAMES, Unity Consciousness and Separation Consciousness:

This is where the concept of twin flames can help us understand our true nature. As source energy, God or I AM, we are pure positive energy, anode, with an ever-flowing nature. To be born here on earth, we need a Twin Flame, which can also be referred to as Twin Energy, to act as our opposite, a cathode. This is how we are able to experience self, through contrast, a condition of this planet.

To review, the theory goes that we agree to have an exact imprint of our energy in another body, which operates as our polar opposite, a cathode, who also incarnates. This is the only way we can have a human experience, otherwise we would just be in flow state or anode. The birth of the twin flame theory is rooted in the teachings of **separation consciousness**. Separation consciousness has its purpose: so we can incarnate and explore a physical existence.

Oversimplified, if the flames stay in **separation consciousness**, not knowing they are "One" in The ALL, they will always feel like the back sides of magnets towards each other (anode/cathode) after the initial ecstasy phase. However, if they, while incarnated, learn **unity consciousness**, their own **oneness** with everything, knowing they are a part of The ALL, then they will rejoice in a powerful relationship.

Thousands of people get stuck thinking they need their twin to feel complete. Flames are whole energies and do not need to complete each other or even meet on the physical level. The teaching here is for all of us to seek to transcend **separation consciousness** and feel complete, part of The All, and experience **unity consciousness**, which is our true nature. In ancient and recent texts, this is referred to as "The Human Flowering."

Achieving unity consciousness with or without a twin flame does not mean we will be without challenge. We came here to experience contrast, and indeed, that is how we feel alive. Embracing our own shadow work and bringing it into the light allows us to live a deeper and more meaningful existence because it fuels our compassion for fellow humans who are suffering.

Neale Donald Walsch writes in *What God Said,* "Your life has nothing to do with you. It is about everyone whose life you touch and how you touch it." Before Shadow Work, when we are in pain, we do not have a healthy enough capacity to be in service to others.

After Shadow Work, we go from disconnected helpless human (separation consciousness), to "God" OR I AM in action (unity consciousness).

We are not the human condition, we are the awareness of the human condition.

I AM:

The term I AM works well to explain this life energy that comes from the ALL and flows through us because it is impossible to hold a phrase like "I AM" as separate from ourselves.

This energy is not just out there, it's everywhere, inside and out and all around. It's also dark matter, which in spiritual circles is referred to as "mind," meaning the thoughts of the Universe, God's essence, and our essence exist in all things and creates all things. We are an expression of source energy, and we are source energy.

The Purpose:

Our life's essence or experiences get inserted into The ALL and make it possible for others to experience it as well. So if you've had a terrible upbringing but work through it and are graced with internal (there's that word again) forgiveness and flow, then 200 years from now, since that energy has been expressed through you, someone else can access that healing or blessing.

We are giving through living. I take this to be the meaning of Erin's title, *One Truth, One Law: I AM, I CREATE*. There is no wrong way to create in the big picture. Anode or Cathode, it is all a contribution, and it all matters. We are creators.

Quiet the mind:

We were not abandoned on some rock and let loose to survive on our own. We were given all we need to thrive, and it's within us, fully accessible when we "quiet our minds."

This is why everyone teaching on the path for thousands of years encourages us to meditate twice a day. Meditation itself burns up disbelief and incinerates untruths to make way for real reality.

Real reality is we are all God in action, Source Energy, or I AM. It does not matter what we call it, and any individual title will never fully explain what it is anyway, but it is all there is, and we are that. Quiet the mind and "see" for yourself.

Stop resisting and start flowing:

It's not necessary to live a linear life of suffering. One major key is to learn to **flow without resisting the ups and downs**, and observe. Understand that you are what observes, not the thoughts you are thinking.

Resisting is the foundation of suffering. As we flow, meditate and connect with our core of energy, the internal knowing Love and Wisdom, guides us out of suffering.

Rajada told me to pinch my arm really hard, just short of drawing blood. Wanting the lesson, I did what he said.

"Now stare deeply into it, don't resist, feel the pain, go right to the center and observe, then tell me what happens."

After a moment, wide eyed, I barked, "The pain vanished!"

The lesson on the path has never been to avoid our feelings or pain. The idea is to go deep enough into whatever you are resisting and allow it to fully express with your supervised permission. By no means are we saying to get in there and think, think, think, creating more and more suffering. Let's not unpack our bags and live there, but to allow and align with our inner knowing/I AM to gently guide us in those moments, and then out of them.

Our concentrated focused energy continues to create beyond us:

Every major decision point, doubt or thought given lots of energy in our lives spins off into other energetic expressions or entities. If I wanted to marry that Rock Star, but was internally redirected for a little league type father, that "life" or concentration of energy, still expresses beyond me. Sounds crazy, right? We do not have to ponder regret anymore. Everything really is happening all at once.

Take a look at the movie "Everything, Everywhere, All at Once." As Michelle Yeoh's character freaks out, illustrated like a pane of glass, she breaks apart into all the other aspects of herself. That is actually a concept of Maha Kali, a Hindu Goddess. Folklore has it Kali gets angry at Shiva; she busts out into all of her different aspects and demands to be known as whole. She becomes extremely powerful and all-knowing, giving birth to Maja Kali. Finally, she truly knows herself.

All of our aspects get to be expressed, just not in the linear idea we have created through being human.

Just because we can't see it, doesn't mean it's not happening:

To some that will sound crazy, but think of a fan that is still. We see the blades clear as day, but turn on the fan and the blades become invisible. Even though the blades are invisible we know they are there right in front of us. These energy expressions are like that, existing in a different frequency so we can't see them. This is so the I AM can continue to know itself and all of its aspects available through us.

This energy does not have the limitation of time:

Our inner being does not have the limitation of time. It powerfully knows how to put us in the right place and right time for whatever it is we want to create, even decades in advance. What if time was no longer a limitation for you? As you meditate, synchronicity comes alive!

Now, because of free will, we also create what we don't want by not fully understanding our own power with this limitless connection, so it serves us to get busy.

We have access:

On the fun side, if you want to channel Picasso's essence into your art, you can, as long as you have access to your inner being. Welcome to the biggest shopping store in the Universe, where the only currency is our connection through a quiet mind, centered in the now.

We will never understand it, so free your mind of trying:

We will never understand what this energy is. For the human brain to figure it out, is like an ant deep in the earth understanding how animals glow thousands of feet below on the ocean floor. We are not meant to know, we are simply meant to create.

Know yourself at the I AM level:

When we upgrade ourselves by contacting our inner knowing, the inner entity, or God, we upgrade The ALL, so everyone, everything, and every situation gets a lift, and humanity evolves. We have a real purpose here.

The Journey to Wholeness

The ALL, I AM, "God", Source Energy

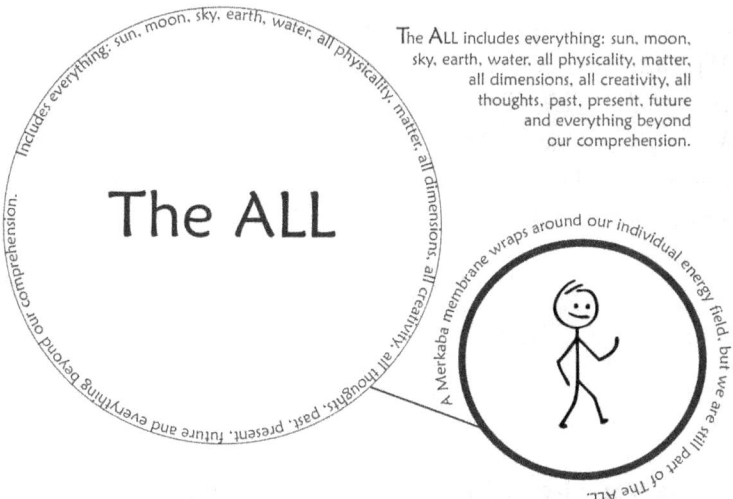

The ALL includes everything: sun, moon, sky, earth, water, all physicality, matter, all dimensions, all creativity, all thoughts, past, present, future and everything beyond our comprehension.

When we incarnate we develop a persona, a separate self, so we can experience the physical world.

The Separated Self Creates

In Separation Consciousness we create countless aspects/energy entities through the decisions we make, the lives we live, the thoughts we think, and the major crossroads we encounter. This is so The ALL can multiply its experience through us.

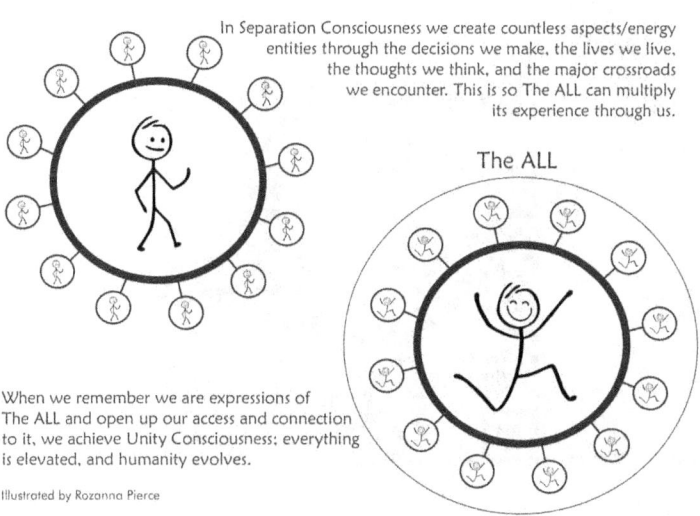

When we remember we are expressions of The ALL and open up our access and connection to it, we achieve Unity Consciousness; everything is elevated, and humanity evolves.

Illustrated by Rozanna Pierce

Although others were initially offended by my people-pleasing healing journey, I moved through the shadows into the light by aligning with my inner entity, I AM. Now, I have an abundance of energy and love to give without agenda.

We can now understand Aristotle's quote, "Knowing yourself is the beginning to all wisdom."

When we achieve Unity Consciousness, we can sense ourselves in others, feel the core of love and wisdom within, and know we have always been whole.

With great love, Your Sister.

Exercise #1: The I AM meditation digital recording
Here's a nifty QR code for a recorded, guided meditation to assist you in asking your I AM questions.

If you do not have a computer handy, here's that exercise in print:
I AM communication exercise
Do this exercise when you are not tired.

Write down two questions you would like to ask the I AM and set aside.
Lay down or sit in a comfortable seat where you can go limp.
Take a breath in for a count of four.
Hold the breath for a count of four.
Let the breath out for a count of four.
Hold the breath out for a count of four.
Imagine you enter a room filled with light, with your mind's eye.
In this room you see yourself sitting comfortably in a white chair.
What clothes are you wearing; what is the look on your face?
In this space you are the I AM, and the person sitting in the chair is your human persona.
Take a long deep breath.
The persona, your human self looks at you, the I AM, and wants to ask a question.
What is the question? Breathe deeply and recall the first question you wrote down.
Now, as the I AM, take a deep breath in, and on a long exhale, receive the answer, not from your head, but from your awareness.
What is the answer? Write one word down to remind you of the answer.
Remain loose and open as the I AM, staying in receiving mode.
Allow "her" to ask the second question from the chair.
As the I AM, again, take a long deep breath in and on the exhale, allow the answer to come to you from your awareness.
What is the answer? Again, write down one word to remind you of the answer.

You have just opened up communication with your inner being!

Congratulations! Does it feel wonky, and maybe not right, like the answer came from your brain and not your I AM? That is normal (!), but now you know how to practice, and you will get better at deciphering the difference between your thoughts and the love and wisdom of your I AM. **A key factor is your inner being will speak in the positive, always, and**

never produce harm to self or others. It will also feel right.

With time, you will be able to have an open dialog with your internal being, your I AM, without the questions, but questions are a great way to begin. You will also improve your alignment automatically as you practice. Enjoy this new dimension of talking to your true "Self".

<u>Exercise #2: A Chant</u>
Put your right fist over your heart and rest your left hand over the top. Speak quietly in a state of blissful receiving.
Be ever faithful to the Great Light Within, the 'Glorious I AM Presence.' Always ask, and then listen for your Inner Guidance, It will and must come clearly, definitely, and correctly.
From *The Magic Presence*, THE GREAT COMMAND

Penny Sisley

Penny Sisley is a Certified Life Coach (CHPC), Modern Mystic and a Cellular Resonance Quantum Healer (CRQH). As the founder of Advanced Life Mastery, she offers womens' energy groups, group coaching, book clubs, and international mentorships. Utilizing CRQH, Tapping, and the ancient art of Shakti Wisdom, she guides women to balance their energy body, shedding layers of cultural, ancestral and DNA dysfunction. Her clients awaken to the I AM within; seeker becomes Source, and a foundational shift occurs. From this new perspective, life becomes an inspiring and expansive journey, where true heart action and bliss can spring. Penny is also an Executive Producer for the film, "America's First Guru," a project dear to her heart.

When she's not leading inspired groups for Gals, you can find her cooking, spending time with her family, or celebrating life with her girlfriends.

https://www.meetup.com/Inspirational-Book-Club-for-Gals/
https://www.advancedlifemastery.com/
psisley@sbcglobal.net
https://www.instagram.com/pennysisley/?hl=en
https://www.linkedin.com/in/penny-sisley/
https://vimeo.com/863725158

EIGHT

A Cinderella Story

Kim Paget

We often think of shadow work with a stab of fear and a heavy feeling in our heart, with work to be started that we would rather avoid at all costs. The reality is yes, it's hard. But, the reality of no growth is harder. To remain stagnant and repeating behaviour and patterns that do not serve you is much more exhausting.

What do you conjure in your mind when you hear the term shadow work? For those who are familiar with it, there may be a feeling of dread at the prospect of delving in. Do I really want to poke around in those places and raise feelings that I am over? What's the point now, anyway?

Shadow work is a deeply personal exercise and is unique to everyone. Sure, we may share similar shadows, but we have them due to our unique situations and circumstances. Whilst the shadow may be the same, the way in which we have embedded it into our psyche can be quite different. Our shadows are like programs installed on our hard drive. We clear our computers from time to time, we find those old games or apps that we don't use anymore, and most of the time we have forgotten they are even there! We go through our system and remove them. They serve no purpose and take up valuable memory.

A Cinderella Story

I was six years old when my mother took me to see Cinderella. We had on our best dresses and made the trip into the heart of Sydney, just Mum and I. It is the first memory of just being with Mum and I together by ourselves; that in itself was special. We found our seats, and I remember looking around and being overwhelmed by the size and absolute opulence of this beautiful old theatre. To my six-year-old eyes, this was a palace. It literally made every little girl who was there feel like a little princess herself!

Then, the movie started, and a program was installed. Usually, when we think of shadow work, we think of the events in our lives that were upsetting, traumatic, and life-changing. We rarely think of an event such as a movie outing. Shadows are programs we have installed on our hard drive. We don't actively install them, but they become installed just the same.

When we decide to work on our shadows, we look for what triggers us, the trauma we have, and where it came from. A special day would not be the first place we look.

What program was installed when I left that theatre all those years ago? *Life will get hard and you may think there is no hope in the situation you find yourself in, but if you work hard and be a good girl, your Prince will come and take you away from all of this! It doesn't matter how much you may think there is no hope, just be patient and put up with what you shouldn't because, in the end, it will be beautiful.* This is a common theme in these classic movies.

This program was very easy to install. The emotions of a day like this can be just as powerful as the emotions of a very bad day. Our brain records this euphoria for a playback many many times. What we remember the most are the powerful memories, good or bad, the events that leave a mark on our hearts. This was a perfect day and thus remembered on some level for the rest of my life.

So I went about my life, and I grew up. I have no memory of actively thinking of this day at the theatre so long ago, but unbeknownst to me, it really had taken up a good chunk of real estate. You have to kiss a few frogs before you find your Prince—so many reminders in everyday life. The program is unaltered from the day it was installed, and society reinforces it around you. Bad relationship? Doesn't matter he obviously was not the "one", but he will come.

What we fail to realise here is the pressure we put on our prospective "Princes" or "Princesses". It's their job to save us and take us away from these "horrible" circumstances we may have found ourselves in. It keeps being reinforced. We all remember the scene in *An Officer and a Gentleman* when Richard Gere sweeps in and picks up Debra Winger and takes her out of the factory she is working in.

So I waited for my Prince to come. Luckily for me, that did not take long. Unluckily for him, he unknowingly had the weight of my expectations on his shoulders. I did not think about the Prince having any issues. Why would he? He is the Prince! We all have our expectations, our boxes that need ticking. The "one" will tick all these boxes and we live happily ever after, right!?

Wrong! Life is a journey with many many lessons along the way, and happiness is an inside job. The weight of being there to make someone else happy is another shadow in itself, but one we rarely look at. Relationships take work. You do not just go back to the castle and live out your days in bliss, which is in direct contrast to the program.

This is a program that has been installed for a very long time and will keep being reinforced by society and ourselves again and again. The problems start when we can't see past this. The program leaves no room for doubt. We believe this is how it is supposed to be.

Shadow work helps us clear the programs that have been installed before we are old enough to rationalise the situation. If someone tells you when you are young that you are not good enough, you don't argue this fact. You believe it to be true and install the program. When you are pigeonholed as a child–oh, you are not the athlete in the family–program installed. Shadow work is finding and removing this software off the hard drive that should never have been there to begin with.

In my years as a tarot reader, the importance of shadow work became abundantly clear to me. Time after time, people find themselves in situations, patterns, and cycles and do not know how to get out of them. They can't believe the same things keep happening to them. They do not take promotions. They do not take new opportunities that come their way. They do not try out for the local football team. Why would they? They have installed "not good enough".

This made me extremely passionate about shadow work. The need to uninstall these programs was essential to allow people to see themselves and what they are truly capable of. This is only possible when the expectations they have installed have been removed. I was so passionate that I created my own oracle deck, Unveiled. Unveiled is a shadow deck; it will help you unveil your shadows that have been lurking in the dark, the programs you have no idea that have been installed.

Of course, I could not help anyone without helping myself first, so my shadow journey began as I began writing Unveiled. When you start to look at your life with fresh eyes, suddenly things become very clear. You can see your own patterns and cycles, and you start to dig. You dig as far as you can until you hit the gold. The gold!!! Yes, the gold! It is here in the dark that you learn what has been holding you back, the obstacles you yourself have imposed, and the magical alchemy begins.

Suddenly, the world looks different. What you considered to be factual is, in fact, a fairytale in itself. Parts of yourself are stripped back, and the truth is like a shining beacon in the dark. You start to understand that someone's opinion and off-handed comment are really not the truth. You can put yourself in another's shoes and see a totally different perspective. You understand projection and start to realise who you really are: who you are, not how others see you.

You realise your programs do not align with the life you desire to live and start actively working through them. You realise when someone uttered "You can't do that", it was from their lens of the world, not yours. You suddenly start healing as the program gets ripped from the hard drive.

Life can actually start to begin again as this beautiful transformation starts to take place. You begin to live the authentic life you were always meant to live. Obstacles become smaller as you become bigger. If you were told, "Children should be seen and not heard" or "Shh, the adults are talking", you slowly begin to get your voice back. You realise you do have value to add to the conversation. We take the good bits or the bad bits, committing them to memory and forgetting the rest.

My Prince and I have been together for thirty-five years. I think we qualify for King and Queen status now! We are not perfect, but we are doing the work, which is far better than a two-dimensional Prince who couldn't even recognise Cinderella. Seriously, he had to tour the town with a shoe, but we all looked past that bit!

If you are new to shadow work you may be thinking, "Where do I start"? This is a great question. I would start with the number 1 card from my Unveiled deck: Accountability. This is a great place to start your journey and will help you become self-aware. This is what it's about, becoming self-aware. Being able to look at yourself from a different perspective. Being able to see your own behaviour and what fuels it.

Accountability is taking responsibility for your actions in any situation. We all play a part, and being aware of your actions is paramount to your accountability. If you understand the reasons behind your actions, you have your answers. When I first started reading tarot, I would always take payment after the reading. One day someone blocked me after the reading, and I had no way of contacting them in regards to payment. This could have gone two ways. I could have gotten angry and upset, or I could think about my part in this situation. My truth was on a subconscious level, if the reading wasn't good enough, then maybe they shouldn't pay for it. Where does this lead? Self-worth.

Take the time to think about some situations in your life and how accountability can help you unveil what actually lies beneath them. This is not an exercise in blame; it is an exercise in self awareness.

As I have explained previously, shadows can hide in places we would never expect. Think about the impact of your own environment and how this may have shaped you and your expectations. I think most of us have watched Friends. Is there a background narrative of "Why don't I have five ride-or-die friends, what's wrong with me"?

We are not computers, and our hard drives cannot be cleaned as easily. But when we put the time and work in, we can clear old beliefs. This work is for you–for you to live a more peaceful life, a life where you have these previous invisible shackles taken off, free to live a life with authenticity, without fear of judgement.

Start right there. In a space of no judgement what would you do?

Feel into this with no restraint.

Now, write down what is actually holding you back from achieving this. This is how you start to take your power back. Take it back from those who you have given it to.

When we fail to "write that chapter" due to the fear of what others may think, they hold the power over our life choices and our path. They are making your choices for you whether you realise this is not. This is when true alchemy starts to happen, when you start to turn this shadow into gold.

You can take your power back. You do not need someone with your shoe in their hand to make it all better. You go shopping and buy a new pair!!!

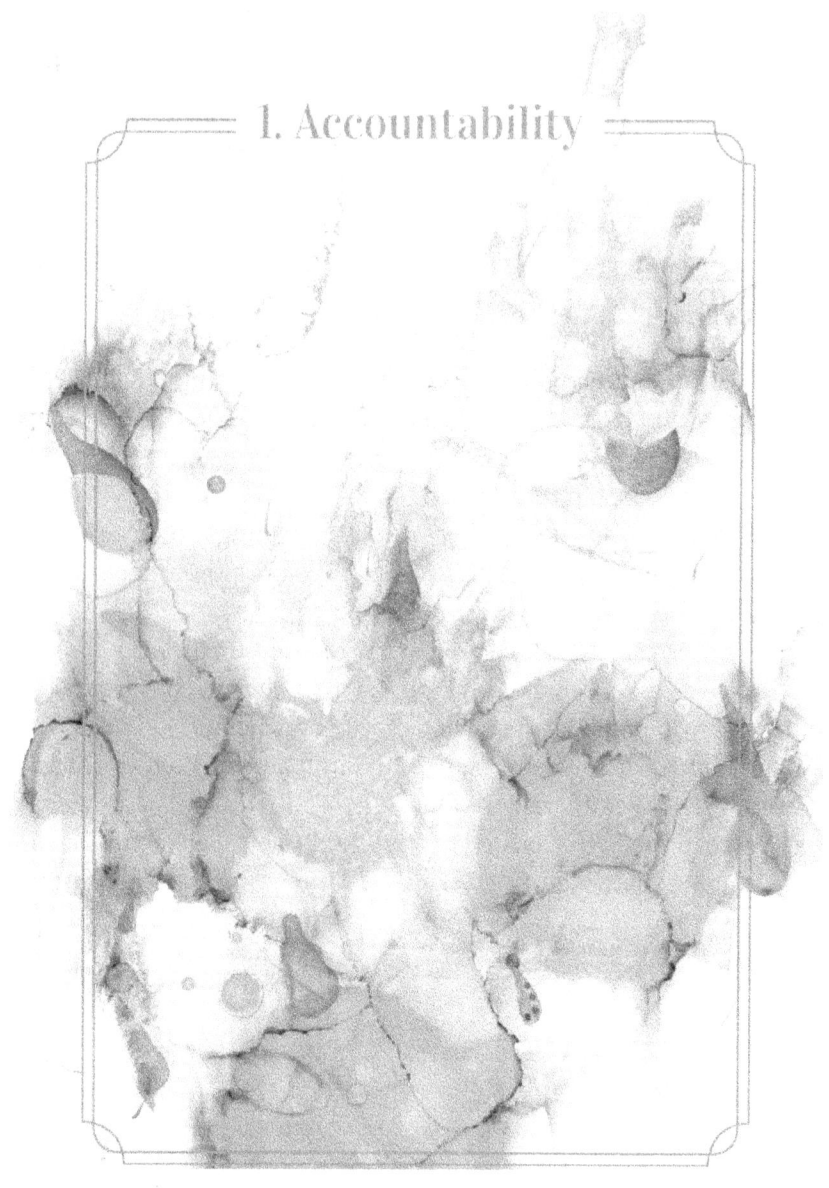

1. Accountability

A Cinderella Story

6. Happiness

An Exercise in Accountability

I have paired the cards Accountability with Happiness from the Unveiled deck. Our happiness is unique to each of us. What one person's happiness may be, can be quite different to others. An exercise in your accountability will lead directly to your happiness.

Look at a situation in your life that is challenging for you right now. What is your part in it? Do you find yourself saying "if I had a better job I would be happy" or "if I lose ten pounds I will be happy". Happiness really does come from within, outside factors will only lead to short term happiness but taking ownership and responsibility for your own choices will help you find the happiness within. If you have a challenging job that is not really suited to you and may even be toxic but you refuse to leave, this is your choice. If you are only five years till retirement, this is still your choice to stay. If you would like to drop a dress size but do nothing to achieve this, this is your choice.

If you look at your life you will see the choices you have made that have brought you to this very point in your own life. Taking accountability means looking back without judgment or trying to justify reasons, but actually taking responsibility for these choices.

Look at some of the challenging situations in your life right now and with complete honesty answer the questions below.

• Did I do my best to set clear goals?

• Did I do my best to make progress towards goal achievement?

- Did I do my best to find meaning?

- Did I do my best to be happy?

- Did I do my best to build positive relationships?

Kim Paget

Kim Michelle Paget is the creator and artist of the Oracle deck Unveiled. Kim is an international intuitive Tarot reader and teacher. After many years of reading tarot, she felt the need to bring more self-awareness into the lives of others and thus the Unveiled deck was born. Kim has also studied the Akashic Records, Reiki and Psychic Development.

Kim is also an artist who uses the medium of alcohol ink to channel your unique energy into a one-of-a-kind artwork. Kim is the owner of Tarot, Trinkets & Treasures, an online store which serves her worldwide clientele.

Kim lives in Sydney, at the foot of the Blue Mountains with her family and a house full of animals!

www.tarottrinketsandtreasures.com.au

FB - Tarot, Trinkets & Treasures
    Tarot, Trinkets & Treasures Community Group
    Insta - tarottrinketsandtreasures

NINE

Death and Life/Shadow and Light

Red MoonEagle

Between one gasp of air to the next: there is no breath. I remember the experience vividly. My first asthma attack, I quit breathing. I was 18 months old. Held and touched with harshness, the strident sounds of raised voices around me, and the smell of fear. I remember the emotional quality of the experience of not being loved, fear of not being good enough, being smothered, or not doing the "right" things, and the rejection of unconditional love. I recall having to make the conscious decision to return. My guides were there, showering me with love from the other side, because here, love was scarce. I had to make the choice to come back; the fear of being unloved in this physical realm of suffering had me frozen and not breathing. This marked my first encounter with the shadow essence of Natural Number 6. This was the first experience of the lesson from the wheel of life through the light and shadow. I had to choose to return to this place and see the potential of the light. This was my earliest near-death experience and not the scariest I'd face.

Death and Life/Shadow and Light

Let's Talk About Death, Baby

There is an interesting thing that happens when people talk about near-death experiences with me. As soon as I talk about my own dying, they become startled, then horrified, then aghast, then disbelieving. It's okay. I don't mind. I know that death, for many, is a scary thing. What happens beyond that shadowy thing called 'death'?

Death is change. Death is a transformation from one state into another, much like the law of conservation of energy, which states that energy is neither created nor destroyed. When people use energy, it doesn't disappear. Energy changes from one form into another.

How Can I Be Certain?

I can only know my own shadow-light, light-shadow journey. Though there were ten death experiences in my life, I will be focusing on a few specific stories that illustrate the layered complexity and meaning of the journey of shadow and light through the Wheel of Life. Recently, there has been more clarity of why within the understanding of Shadow/Light Work through the lens of Body of 9 and Natural Numbers. This is an exciting next phase of my own journey as a catalyst and Healer's Teacher. There is nothing to fear; there is only love.

I have witnessed too many people in my life reject the lessons of shadow and light. Too many people stayed caught in the whirlpool of karma, rejecting the complexities of shadow and light. Instead, they chose the "easy" way: the perceived "happiness" which kept them caught in misery and unhappiness. Their lives became facsimiles of society where those outside themselves told them happiness should/could/would be. They implemented "only the light," rejecting the shadows, and lost themselves.

Conversely, I learned to lean into the shadow and light cycle, share, and overshare. I learned to teach about the shadow through the symbols, patterns and stories. The stories of our ancestors from around the world connected us to the wisdom of shadow and light. I learned to lean into authentic exploration of that cycle, that flow, that waning and waxing journey. I learned that sharing joy, rather than fear, would catalyze in others their own journey. Teaching this continually for nearly 30 years opened the doors to my next journey, which is why we are here today, in this moment, learning with each other about the alchemical transformation of shadow work.

Learning the Language

Every Body of 9 Natural Number posture-perfect activation holds a fundamental frame of understanding of the world and creates a new perspective. This informed perspective reflects in your thoughts, actions, and reactions in life, shaping your core investment in reality, the strength of your natural presence in this world. Within the Body of 9 community, this informed viewpoint is hailed as a "superpower," beautifully and precisely exemplifying the manifestation of the "light" within our natural presence.

Every natural presence maintains a balance of light and shadow, serving as the fundamental forces that orchestrate the interplay between oneself and the reality we collectively share. The shadow side cannot be ignored; it is essential in the completeness of the natural physiological activation because it is your emotional core investment in reality, potentially highlighting the emotional significance and connection in this realm.

These forces are not categorized as strong or weak, good or bad, but rather represent the established, natural flow of each activation within the body. Flow cannot happen if you are not moving; flow is not bidirectional or linear. Flow is multidimensional, quantumly connected, and now, here, you. The ancient teachings of the Wheel of Life are always circling: mind, spirit, emotion, body, all surrounded by community, the connection to each other.

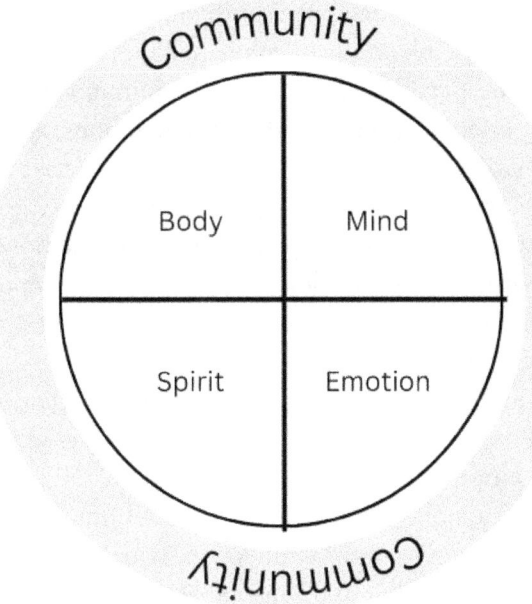

Death of the Heart: Finding My Place of Peace

When I was a teenager, I died during heart surgery. At that time, I was deeply and overwhelmingly in love with my boyfriend, Sam. The connection I shared with Sam was one of the deepest I had experienced up to that point in my life, encompassing past-life connections, soul awareness, and a sense of timelessness. We were often seen together and told that our smiles joined in our joy would light up space and make everyone around us brighten; conversely, if we could not bring our smiles forward, the room to others would seem dark and heavy. Through my connection with Sam, I confronted the light and shadow of the depth of my darkest fears, my fear of connecting with others and the purpose of human connection.

The surgery should have been pretty straightforward, and for most, it probably is. In my case, the radio frequency used to "burn" off the tissue caused atrial fibrillation and a spasm of the heart, and the tool punctured the upper aorta, creating further complications.

The physiological experience, melded the fear of physical pain, and the emotional hurts, blending together to be a large "monster" of fear. Sam was the person I knew I could communicate the intricacies of that experience, the depth of all the emotions, as well as trust to the monster of embodied fear that came from that experience. Sam was very much a part of my journey for the next 8 years. Through the gauntlet of life and death, he taught me how to hold in sacred trust that joy of connection, the depth of the imperfection of that love, and the focus to move forward, until we were able to release each other to our individual purposes.

It was through this near-death and the ensuing shadow journey that I was able to "settle" into the purpose of my life, understanding the reason for emotional connections to each other. This experience brought all the fears and losses associated with human connection—fears of finding my own inner connection, fears of imperfection in relationships, taking risks, and the capacity for connection with others. Amidst those shadows, I discovered the light, finding a supreme sense of peace and joy in connection. That death was pivotal because within it, I unearthed the place of peace in light and the shadow inherent in the death of my body's Natural Number 3, located in the upper chest, centered at the manubrium.

Losing My Wisdom: Finding the Divine Source

The next experience with death was probably one of the worst and linked to Natural Number 1, or the throat. The shattering depth of this emotional shadow work, which took many years to untangle fully, was because of the toxic relationship with my biological mother. The extraction of my wisdom teeth and the subsequent severe medical reaction, culminated in my death and then coma.

I remember going "under," and nothing but layers of emotion until waking a week later, feeling the painful spasms of my throat muscles, esophagus and larynx from the tube. As I came into wakefulness and consciousness, the layers of shadow welled up as I tried to fight the tubes, the pain and the shame. The overwhelming waves of shame from a perceived lack of perfection and not feeling good enough. As the nurses rushed in, at the call of someone in the room, "She's awake," I heard a voice telling me, "Don't fight it." The voice was filled with judgment, perfectionism, and worries about what others would think. However, the moment I died, I heard the voice of "god" and "goddess," realizing within that shadow that I am loved and possess the capacity to embody the divine.

This death propelled me into making pivotal choices necessary to truly embrace my life's path and trust. I began to trust the divine within myself, recognizing that I am loved and the presence of my earthly mother may not be as necessary as I once believed. I began the untangling of those voices in my life, that forced their own shame, perfection, and judgment toward me.

Death of Isolation: We Need One Another

Though it took three more years to fully realize the influence of that experience, it marked the beginning of delving deeper into the layers of light and shadow work needed for me to truly embody myself in this earthly existence.

The next death was a genuine death experience, far removed from family, friends, and support networks, and the shadows cast by it were profoundly influential. Though driven to break away from my biological family, I did not have the tools to create the needed community. This second death of the Natural Number 2, settled in the upper abs, was catastrophic and not pleasant to review in detail. It brought an all-encompassing disappointment in meeting the expectations of others, as well as in disappointing myself and my guides. I was so isolated from purpose and connections. It was a journey of recognizing the disappointment in failing to navigate the path of shadow effectively and not acknowledging the depth and strength of my own light. I shed buckets of tears for weeks leading up to my body's death, tears of not being able to mirror back what was needed the "right" way to make connections.

This death brought the shadow of learned discernment of when to say no and when to say yes, guided by higher purposes rather than the expectations of others. I allowed myself to acknowledge that others' disappointments need not become my own. I had to learn to recognize my light and my shadow and to allow others to be themselves without my shadow interfering.

Death of Alone: The Entities Within

Several years of separation from my biological family, coupled with the completion of a blueprint contract to bear more children from this human body, led me to choose sterilization through tubal oblation. The allergic reaction to medications resulted in a near-death experience, thereby severing my connection to this body's Natural Number 4, located in the lower abdomen.

There is a sense of timelessness with death and near death, such that it could have taken place yesterday, is still happening today, and will have an impact in the future. Timelessness of emotions and the emotional shadows I traversed in severing and disconnecting from generational contracts brought feelings of relief and a deep honoring of the authenticity of my own purpose. I felt the threaded connections through my body, following the entities within, through the layers of ancestral connections. I felt the love and honor I have for my grandmother and great-grandmothers and the love of those memories through time from them. Earth Herself threaded into the joy, translucence of knowing, and the joyousness of my ability to acknowledge their gifts through those connections. I traversed the love, joy, and bliss to the release of all of their shame, fear and disappointments. It became safe to live this life. With the snip-snip of my tubes, I snip-snipped the ties to ancestral traumas.

Death of Self: Refusal to Participate

The final journey towards near-death was my attempted suicide. This death is significant because of the difference from all the others. The despair and overwhelming dread of having no way to move forward was crippling. All I wanted was to go "home." Through breathless sobs and choked anguish, I felt trapped in the events that led up to this point: the betrayal of those I trusted and loved, being abandoned by friends, and the bleak shadowy darkness to come. It felt as though the universe spent decades trying to break my bodily connections to this world, now it was my turn to say, "Fuck you!" By leaving, I would punish those who caused me pain, and somehow also release them. Nothing I seemed to touch or do was the right thing. The world was not ready for me, so I chose to leave.

The existential dread of living without purpose, coupled with the realization of my purpose entwined with time, death, and rebirth, destabilized my entire existence. This learning from overwhelming despair to the light upon waking served as preparation for the Dark Time ahead. This marked the death of Natural Number 7, or the third eye, within my body.

The Lessons of Death: the Shadow/Light Transformation

The death of Natural Number 7 was the journey back. I had to choose life in the Wheel of Life in body, mind, spirit, emotion, and connection to the community of humanity. Throughout my life, I have experienced the death of all nine Natural Numbers. The truth is that through the journey of shadow and light the revelation that the beauty of the light is juxtaposed to the challenge of the shadow. It has given me a road map for living through my perceptive abilities in a whole new way. The journey from death back to life may seem random, but the divine brilliance of the event's patterns within the Wheel becomes evident when connected.

Body of 9 gave me the context for understanding the experiences of all ten deaths and the transformation of my own experiential transformational flow that changed my body. Learning to embody all the Natural Numbers, I learned to understand the lessons of each death and integrated the experiences, and now can honor that wisdom in my body. When I learned to activate Natural Number 8 through that training, all the experiences of those deaths were integrated into my body in a way that had not been present before.

The death of NN6, steeped in fear of not being loved right now, led to the death of NN3 and the joy we bring to one another. This paved the way for the death of NN1 and the divine connection inherent in us all. The death of NN2 reinforced the need for community, connection and honoring each other just as we are, and myself in this Wheel of Life, most of all. This sequence then led to the deaths of NN4 and NN7: the shadow of self and the vastness of potential outcomes and the choices to participate or not.

The biggest lesson of all is not for me. The lesson is for you. These near-death experiences of shadow and light are not necessary for you to open the doors of the shadow and journey through to the other side to find the light within the shadow. Your journey can begin simply. Experience the activation of your own natural physiological power center, lean into the light and shadow, and then open the doors to all the others. This is an opportunity to explore the fun, joy, and bliss through transformation of shadow to light, and light to shadow.

Let's journey the Wheel of Life through actions:

1. Water (the physical place in the Wheel): Water is life. Take a glass of water and hold it in your hands. Focus your thoughts on "charging" the water with light. Ask the water to go to all the cells of your body that hold Shame, Fear of Disappointment. Ask the water to flow through that shadowed emotion and bubble it up so you can consciously let it go. Drink your water. Feel the light flow through and in you, touching all parts of your body, infusing with the light of life and joy or water.

2. Food (the community connection surrounding the Wheel): Eat real food. Avoid food-like substances. Charge your food, like above. Allow the food to nourish your cells, and invite your body to take the energy from that food to work through the shadows of emotion and pain that have found ways to hide out in your cells. Eat with people who connect with you in community. Find ways to share real food, community, connection and social support. We already do this in our culture; we look to the past for clarity on how to do this. Blessings are charging your food, smaller portions, shared amongst many, taking your time to enjoy the flavors, and energy, and allow the body to properly digest the food. Avoid alcohol.

3. Breath (the Spiritual connection of the Wheel): Take a few deep breaths down into your belly, filling your lungs all the way from the bottom with air. Then release, forcing out as fast as you can. Slow breath in, and fast breath out. What are the emotions this triggers? Do you feel the need to move? Is there pain in your body? The breath opens the blood vessels oxygenating your body. When breathing like this, fears in the body can come up. How do you journey through the fear and let it go?

4. Movement(the Mental Being of the Wheel): What does movement look like for you? Is it dance, exercise programs, leisurely walking, hiking up a mountain, or another form? When journeying through the wheel with shadow, use movement to work through the emotional qualities that "shadow" your life. Do you use music and vibration to help you with emotions and movement? Actively move each day; it does not have to be strenuous, just move.

5. Rest (the Emotional being of the Wheel): Ever notice when you are not rested, you are irritable and unable to handle emotions? This is essential for all the areas of the Wheel to come into connection with light and shadow. All aspects of the Wheel have the magnetism of connection to each other, and yet the shadows of each can and will inhibit the movement into light. Even if you are not sleeping 8 hours a night, find time to rest, easing your body and mind. Have you ever taken a break from something emotionally intense and done something else to be able to get back to that emotionally charged thing? That is resting. Resting can look like many different things. Take 15 minutes, 3x a day, and rest in body, mind, spirit, and emotion; drink water, make sure you are fed, take some good deep breaths, and assess your emotional state; take rest as you need it.

Red MoonEagle

Wherever Red touches a life, movement occurs. Red MoonEagle is a conduit for catalyzing energy when people are stuck at an intersection in life. Whether that be in body, mind, spirit, or emotion, her offerings of cascading energy guides you toward who, what, where, and when action is required on your part.

In her practices, she harnesses psycho-spiritual healing techniques, the Body of 9 Natural Number Identification, transformational coaching questions, and the powerful energy work of the biofield. She considers each individual's holistic well-being, addressing the body, mind, energy, frequency, emotions, spiritual growth, and the power of choice. Red collaborates with your spirit guides to unveil your personal blueprints, guiding you toward harmonious acceptance of your life's journey and choices.

Red MoonEagle has worked in the last 30+ years as a teacher in the public and private sectors of education, focusing on diversified learning models and high-risk youth. She also spent time in Management and Leadership in the Hospitality Industry and Alternative Health. Red has successfully turned dysfunctional teams into working, cohesive units, maximizing workplace potential. She has been teaching in the metaphysical world, reaching hundreds of students over 30 years to find successful personal, business, and spiritual balance and overall success through her teachings and coaching.

https://www.elementalhealingmt.com

YouTube: Daily Devotional with Red MoonEagle
https://www.youtube.com/channel/UCzSPbWpJtr3GQRo1e1taffA

Instagram: elemental_healing_mt
arisehealingcenter.com

TEN

Motherhood: An Evolutionary Spiritual Container

Dannie French

It was 3:59 p.m. on Wednesday, 10th July 2019: the day that irrevocably changed my life.

"I need to push," I screamed.

"No, you're not ready yet," said the midwife.

I intuitively knew at that moment my baby was coming, regardless of what the midwife said. I was laying on the hospital bed in the spacious private birthing suite, husband beside me, intensely laser focussing on the serene rainforest wallpaper, breathing with my body as the last contraction shot my son out onto the white sheets beneath me, shocking the midwife at his swift entrance into the world. In that moment, the rush of oxytocin was ecstatic.

I couldn't wait to feel his tiny, warm body connect with my hands. Instantly, I drew him close to my heart for our first-ever cuddle, as he nuzzled his way towards my breast, immediately latching tightly. As I attentively and mesmerizingly observed his first moments of life, we lovingly locked eyes for the first time, my heart cracked wide open and a waterfall of love cascaded into every single cell of my body.

This was the most magical and proudest moment in my whole entire life. A moment I had absolutely no control over, and yet I felt incredibly empowered surrendering to the process: ultimate trust in my body. I had just naturally birthed my son with no synthetic pain relief or interventions, just the magnificent naturally occurring chemicals within my own body. I'd never had such trust in my body before, only a hell of a lot of judgement and shame. What an honour it is to be a woman, create life and birth life through the portal of our womb. What I hadn't yet realised about this life-changing moment was I had just birthed my greatest teacher and spiritual guide, my son Jayde. What I knew for sure, though, was that I was going to raise my son differently from the way I was raised.

Doing things differently is the exact energy that I desired to mother from. I desired to be a calm, compassionate and conscious mother guided by my heart. Growing up, I was raised around women who mothered in an authoritarian style, who believed children should be seen and not heard. Showing your emotions meant you were weak, and if your children didn't behave, it meant you couldn't control your children. I was determined to raise my son without him feeling the heartache and pain I felt as a child when parented under these rigid rules and fear-based beliefs. I was determined to do anything I could to ensure he felt loved, appreciated, and supported in his view of himself, his emotional experiences and his view of the world. I would not repeat the generational cycle of my lineage that taught me showing love, affection and emotions equals weakness. This was my motivation to heal myself.

The first couple of months of early motherhood were very strange and confusing. I remember feeling oddly and indescribably different, like a stranger in my own body. The greatest challenge I faced was grasping my new identity, my new role, and the emotions that came with those changes. When we become mothers, our lives shift so dramatically that we can become confused by the person we are now. Who am I now that I'm a mother?

When I was 19, I worked for Telstra as a retail sales consultant for roughly three years, and if I wasn't leading with the most KPI's every month consecutively, I would consider myself a failure. At this stage in my life, I also struggled with acne on my face. Truthfully, I was so embarrassed, shameful and disgusted by the way I looked. I would wear a thick layer of foundation to try and hide and disguise my revolting pimples. It was my security blanket that gave me the courage to step outside my door. I recall feeling so distressed about my appearance, that I would arrive at Telstra earlier than my start time to choose the consulting desk based on which side of my face was more disgraceful. I'd ensure that the worst side of my face was facing the wall so my customers didn't have to look at it.

In my mid-twenties, I worked for a transport company where I was paid for forty hours but the manager expected fifty hours of work from me, and so I did. I was always striving to be the perfect, polished person and I built a solid and rigid identity around this persona. So what now? I was a stay-at-home mum and had a baby to look after. I was overwhelmed by all the responsibilities. I'd only known how to be a hardworking employee. The uncertainty of my new world was painfully uncomfortable.

I distinctly remember a Monday morning in November 2019. I'd just finished breastfeeding Jayde and popped him into his bouncer on the floor, desperately hoping that this time he would sleep for an hour or more rather than his usual twenty to forty-minute nap. This particular day was day three of continually cluster feeding. I sat next to him on my lounge room floor in an empty, quiet house, hunched over, hugging my legs, chronically sleep-deprived, feeling as though a dark depressive cloud was hovering over my head and pressing down on my shoulders like a heavy rock. Thoughts of defeat filled my mind: 'I don't know what to do', 'I can't do this anymore', 'I'm so tired'.

That's when I felt the substantial weight that comes with being a new mother. I burst into uncontrollable tears. Was my mother right? 'Never have children, they'll ruin your life', 'They'll suck the life right out of you'. Even if she did say it jokingly, those were the words that instantly came to mind in the moment of complete despair. I cried on my floor all alone until I couldn't cry anymore.

Suddenly, in that vulnerable hot mess of a moment on the floor, I had a reconciliation of my life right up until this point. I realised something profound. I had just become consciously aware that I had spent my years thus far worrying about everyone else but myself, putting others first, not expressing my voice, striving and pushing myself to exhaustion and severe headaches to prove my value. I was trying to control everything around me, and for what? Exhaustion, pain and dissatisfaction? For who? Everyone else? I was so consumed by what people thought of me, not for once had I genuinely thought about myself. What do I want? What makes me happy?

That's when I found meditation, or meditation found me. In my eager state to find my own inner happiness, I popped on the podcast show I was bingeing at the time, but somehow I mistakenly clicked on the Crappy to Happy Podcast with Cass Dunn. She was interviewing Tom Cronin on Vedic Meditation. This podcast sparked something spectacular inside of me. I was astounded by the way meditation changed his life.

Feeling equally inspired and bubbling with excitement, I went straight to Tom's website and bought his self-paced meditation course. I followed it religiously, practising two sessions of twenty minutes a day, every day as prescribed. I was astounded at the instant calming effects I felt after my meditation sessions. One particular day, as I was sitting on my soft grey meditation couch, I heard 'reconnect with your dad'. It shocked me, and I was totally surprised as to where those words came from. I trusted and followed the guidance and reconnected with my dad after almost ten years of silence, and the initial meet-up went intriguingly well. I became fascinated by this phenomenon.

I started experimenting with asking a question in meditation and listening attentively, just to see what would happen. Sure enough, I would receive an answer; sometimes it was sentences long and always in such wise, loving and compassionate language. In my enthusiasm and excitement, I started to meditate with a journal beside me so that I could record all the beautiful words I was looking forward to hearing. Every time I practised this new technique, I would eagerly absorb all the encouragement I needed to hear. What was really fucking interesting was that all this guidance was relevant to exactly what I was going through at the time. It felt

Motherhood: An Evolutionary Spiritual Container

as though I had a little cheerleader and supporter sitting on my shoulder, watching over me and guiding me through the dense emotional fog and confusion I was lost in.

I later discovered on a spiritual podcast episode that this was, in fact, my connection to my 'higher self'. As I heard the woman say those words, my eyes opened, I gasped for air like it was the last inhale of my life, and I froze still in my black cane dining room chair.

OH, THAT'S IT! I thought.

Immediately, I ran straight into my study and sat on my comfy grey meditation couch, grabbed my devotional journal and favourite gel ink pen. A gut feeling motivated me to switch things up. This time I sat deep in meditation first. After twenty minutes of connecting with myself, I opened my journal, gripped my pen tightly and watched intently as my pen and hand began creating magic. I started channeling my higher self.

As I sat witnessing this divine connection taking place, tears of joy streamed down my face as every word landed deep in my heart. I realised this was the support, guidance, love, affirmation and encouragement I had always needed and was never receiving externally. It was in that profound moment of pure heart-opening gratitude, I felt a jolt of energy radiating throughout my entire body as I relished in this visceral full-body chill moment. Suddenly, I realised the power of the statement 'everything you need is within you'.

This deep awareness and understanding of those six profound words is what catapulted me into a state of consciousness, where I was fully committed to exploring the depths of my inner emotional world. I began frequently journaling my emotions, feelings and troubles out on paper. I used to do this as a teenager, but only once in my whole twenties. It was the only way I could safely express myself and feel heard. It felt soothing to pick the pen up again and release my inner turbulence.

Roughly a month later, when my son was six months old, I was diagnosed with postnatal depression and anxiety. I sat in the small cold air-conditioned doctor's office, waiting as she pulled my patient file up. My stomach started churning, my legs bouncing uncontrollably, tears welling up in my eyes as I started to fiddle with my fingers and nails waiting for my doctor to share the results.

My doctor said in a soft tone, "You have postnatal depression and anxiety".

I dropped my head into my hands and cried in defeat. I thought to myself, 'What the hell, how did I get here?' 'What do I do now?' 'I have a baby to raise, I can't be in this state!' 'What will people think of me now?'

I chose the path of talking to a psychologist over medication. This was the moment when healing myself and my generational pattern came to the forefront for me.

In 2021, I signed up to study EFT (Emotional Freedom Technique) and Matrix Reimprinting to become a certified Practitioner so I could use these techniques on myself for my own healing. This is where I began to dive deep into releasing all my suppressed and trapped emotions stored in my body and revisit the traumatic memories imprinted into my subconscious mind. It's through this technique and visiting hundreds of my memories that I have been able to bring perspective to my traumatic experiences, which I didn't have access to at the time of trauma. It's helped me to resolve the deep emotions I've been resisting for so long and has supported me to finally find truth and acceptance for myself and my past. This modality has been a crucial, transformational element in my self-acceptance and self-love journey. The impact it's had on me and my clients is truly life-altering.

I vividly remember when I was six, I stole ten dollars out of my cousin's wallet, which I got into so much trouble for with my mother. I was punished and told to personally return the money to my cousin and admit I had stolen it. Using Matrix Reimprinting, I went back and revisited this traumatic memory. What I discovered when I was face to face in this memory with my six-year-old self was her deep feelings of shame, guilt, despair, sadness, powerlessness and rejection. These were all the feelings I was experiencing at that very moment as I burst into tears in front of the doctor when she said I had postnatal depression and also when I was sitting on my lounge room floor months prior.

Motherhood: An Evolutionary Spiritual Container

I recall the loud yelling and rage my mother was feeling when she shamed me for being a 'naughty girl' for stealing my cousin's money. I know that at the time, she didn't mean to hurt me, she was just trying to teach me a lesson so that I wouldn't end up developing a habit of stealing and thinking that was acceptable behaviour. However, as a six-year-old, I felt riddled with guilt, and in that moment, I decided I was a bad person. I was so distressed that I had so deeply disappointed my mother. I was left feeling not good enough, unaccepted and rejected based on my interpretations of the situation at that time.

When I asked my younger self why I had taken the money, she replied, 'Because I loved money, and I'd never had my own.' Clearly, I was not stealing it to be a naughty child. It was from an honest place of possibility and wonder. My core beliefs cemented into my subconscious from this memory were that I am a bad person, I'm not good enough, and I always disappoint people.

What happens in these times of trauma is that we create limiting beliefs based on our perceptions of ourselves, others, and the world. These beliefs are imprinted into our subconscious mind to protect us so we avoid them in the future. Just like when you burn yourself, you very quickly learn that it hurts and that you should not do it again. Based on this awareness, you alter your behaviour to avoid it happening again. Our beliefs are programmed the same way.

Take my example above. We encounter an experience where we learn 'I am a bad person', 'I'm not good enough', and 'I disappoint people.' We perceive that we are not accepted, therefore we fear being rejected by others in the future. To avoid these situations from happening again and the painful emotions they evoke (which we want to avoid feeling at all costs to protect ourselves), we create behavioural adaptations such as perfectionism, people-pleasing and overgiving. It's a way for us to prove to others that we ARE a good person, that we ARE good enough to be liked, and that we WON'T disappoint others again. This is a complete abandonment of self and self-betrayal because you now believe who you are on a fundamental level is not enough. I love this quote by Henry Ford, "Whether you think you can or you think you can't, you're right!"

It all comes down to the power of perception and what you believe.

Ultimately, we are unconsciously moving through life desperately trying to protect ourselves by controlling how others perceive us and convince others that we are, in fact, the opposite of our internal beliefs. This places an immense amount of pressure upon ourselves, in complete rejection and resistance to who we truly are. Rather than coming from an authentic place of genuinely desiring to help someone, these behavioural adaptations come from fear-based beliefs with attachment to proving oneself in order to compensate for our internal resistance to the idea of yourself and feelings of insecurity and inadequacy.

When we can truly feel within us that our perceived inadequacies and insecurities are a lie, just a thought we have chosen to believe, not based on truth, only then do we give ourselves the freedom to experience life through fresh eyes. Once we acknowledge and are willing to feel this suffering deeply, it becomes the gateway to taking our power back. Where we can then take the opportunity to re-parent ourselves in the exact way that we needed as a child so we can give ourselves the spaciousness, grace and access to deep transformation. I believe our inner child doesn't want to be healed; it wants to be heard and held. And, our pain and suffering are our greatest teachers.

I trust with every fibre of my being that my circumstances of life were happening for me, a gift for me to transcend my perceived weakness into my absolute superpower. There's no such thing as fucking it up or getting it right. As a human, you're doing the best you can with what you know or don't know. Once I released the need to prove myself and my worth, I found my humanity. What a weight off my shoulders! An instant sigh of relief. The burden and pressure I'd carried for so long finally dissolved. What I've come to learn and now firmly believe: whatever we perceive as our weakness when transmuted and accepted is actually our greatest superpower! So if you too struggle with low self-worth, I'm here to remind you, your greatest superpower, once realised and owned, is your inherent abundance of true worthiness!

Oceans of love and acceptance,
Dannie xo

1. <u>Life Awareness Building Exercise:</u>

I believe your awareness is your SUPERPOWER!

Learning to cultivate conscious awareness has been the number 1 most powerful tool I have used on my personal transformational journey.

This very practice has allowed me to shift from being on autopilot, totally consumed by my negative thoughts, emotions and reacting in impulsive, unconscious, and unhelpful ways...

To being able to separate from my thoughts and emotions to pause before reacting so that I can observe, invite curiosity and CHOOSE how I wish to respond next.

Find a quiet, comfortable space where you won't be distracted, and have your pen and paper ready.

What recurring themes or parts of your life right now are causing you stress or dissatisfaction (career, relationships, health, money, love, etc.)?

What are the thoughts you have about this situation?

What emotions do those thoughts bring up for you?

What do these emotions stop you from doing, or how do you act in response to these emotions?

What are these circumstances revealing to you about yourself?

What are these circumstances trying to teach you?

What is the overall lesson or truth here?

Now I am aware, what will I CHOOSE to do next time to honour myself when these circumstances arise again?

2. <u>5 Steps to Processing Your Emotions</u>

Step 1: <u>Recognise an emotion is present.</u>
STOP what you are doing and **BE PRESENT** with yourself and the emotion/s.

When you allow yourself to just **FEEL**, you are NOT creating resistance to the feeling.

It's our resistance to feeling emotions that create the barriers stopping them from moving through us like they are supposed to.

(Remember: 'What we resist, persists').

Emotion = Energy in motion.

Therefore, they are meant to move through us, not get stored within us!

Step 2: <u>Breathe.</u>
As a yoga teacher, I know the absolute value and power of the breath and its role in our health and well-being.

The breath is FREE and is the most underrated technique you can use as your very own nervous system regulation tool, that shifts your state almost immediately.

Breathe in through the nose slowly for 4 counts and breathe out through the nose slowly for 8 counts, for a total of 10 rounds (or more if needed).

This breathing technique is a down-regulating breath that will allow you to calm your nervous system and shift you back into the parasympathetic state (rest, digest, and rejuvenate).

Step 3: Acknowledge.

Now that you have become present with the emotion, felt it, and used your breath as a tool to calm your heightened nervous system down, you are now ready to acknowledge it.

Say to yourself or write in a journal, **"I notice I am feeling... (anger)"**

It's important to use this EXACT statement WORD for WORD.

Why?

Because you are now using language that is coming from the perspective of the observer rather than the perspective of being consumed by and becoming the emotion when we say, "I AM ANGRY."

This is a very small change in language but a powerful and profound shift in your psyche, perception and emotional state.

NEVER UNDERESTIMATE THE POWER OF WORDS!

Step 4: Acceptance.

In my experience, allowing yourself to feel and accept your emotions as they become present is the fastest way to process and transcend them.

Without judgement, simply just notice the sensations, colours, textures, temperature of the emotion present within your body and where.

Don't try to change how you feel or rush yourself through it and wish it to be over.

LET IT BE OK that you notice that you are feeling anger.

Sit with the anger and be present with it.

Say to yourself: "I accept that right now I am feeling (anger), and I allow it to be ok. I know this will pass."

Step 5: Enquiry.

We cannot go through an enquiry process whilst we are in the heat of our emotion.

Why?

When we are overwhelmed by our emotions, the amygdala is hijacked (the amygdala is the part of the brain that activates the fight/flight response).

We then operate from our emotional part of the brain (the limbic system), this survival override impairs our rational brain (prefrontal cortex).

This explains why, when our toddlers are in the middle of a meltdown, they cannot take in any information, and you cannot rationalise with them.

We are the same.

So it's important to only answer these questions once you are calm and relaxed state.

Self-enquiry questions:
What is underneath this emotion?
What is this emotion revealing within me?
When have you experienced this emotion before? What transpired?
What was my assumption about the situation that caused this emotion to arise?
What is the need that is not being met here?
How can I meet this need for myself?

3. Inner Child Connection Exercise

Ensure you allow yourself uninterrupted time and space to do this exercise.

Allow your inner child's responses to be fully expressed rather than rush through them.

Ideally, doing this exercise daily will strengthen your connection. You will also discover your unmet needs on a daily basis so you can go ahead and meet them without them piling up.

You can start with...

Hi sweetheart,

I am you from the future and I am writing this letter with the intention to build our relationship together. I am connecting with you to let you know that everything is going to be ok, because I am now here for you every step of the way. I am here to re-parent you in exactly the way you needed. I promise to be here for you always and provide you with the love, acceptance, support, safety and compassion that you need.

What is on your mind today? (Write down their response).

How are you feeling today? (Write down their response).

Would you like me to listen to you or give you some advice/encouragement/or hold you? (Write down the response and give them what they need by either writing it out or giving them a hug: by hugging yourself, a teddy, or a pillow imagining it is little you).

What else do you need to express to me? (Write down their response).

How can I best support you today? (Write down their response and action that they need).

What boundaries can I set for you so you feel safe? (Write down the response and the action they need.)

I want you to know...

I am here for you. I accept you. I understand what you are saying. It's ok to feel what you are feeling. All your emotions are welcome here. All your emotions are valid. I see you. I hear you. I care about you. You are safe. I am proud of you. It's safe to be you. I've got you.

(Insert anything else that you would like your inner child to know).

Thank you for sharing all of you with me.

With love, gratitude and care always...

(Your name) xo

Dannie French

Dannie French is an Emotional Freedom Coach, EFT & Matrix Reimprinting Practitioner, Reiki Energy Healer, Yoga Teacher and psychic medium, otherwise known by her friends as an edgy, powerful pixie who always brings her amazing high vibe energy and infectious smile everywhere she goes. Dannie radiates a warm and compassionate energy that instantly makes you feel seen, safe and comfortable.

Dannie's reclamation of self began at age 31 when the birth of her son sparked a spiritual awakening, leading her into a profound inner journey towards radical acceptance. Dannie is dedicated to a lifelong journey of self-development, soul expansion and contributing to raising global consciousness as a beautiful byproduct and ripple effect of her own transformation.

Growing up as a passionate dancer and performer, Dannie is obsessed with musical theatre and cabaret shows, sequins, red lipstick and dancing up a storm! Her mission is to inspire you to **CHOOSE YOU** and learn to love and accept yourself. Dannie's expertise is listening, shifting your perspective and going deep into recoding and rewiring the subconscious mind so you can jazz up and discover who the fuck you are! Dannie's superpower is her intuitive ability to be deeply self-aware in the moment and is a mad scientist in terms of her own self-exploration.

As an empathetic Emotional Freedom Coach and spiritual mentor, Dannie holds an intentional, sacred and all-accepting space for you to unravel and remember the amazingness of who and what you are so you can sparkle, shine, and radiate love everywhere you go!

Dannie lives on the sunny Gold Coast in Australia with her husband Dean, son Jayde, and two mischievous, adorable Dalmatians. Her ideal day to herself includes sitting on the top of Cabarita or Burleigh Hill, staring out over the Pacific Ocean which inspires her appreciation for the expansiveness life has to offer us in every moment. If she's not on the Hill, she'll be hidden in a quiet shady spot in Currumbin Valley by the flowing waterfalls and bubbling, rocky, crystal clear streams to read, journal and appreciate the peacefulness and serenity the lush rainforest has to offer.

Dannie's Links:
www.danniefrench.com.au
linktr.ee/dannie.french
Instagram: https://www.instagram.com/dannie.french/
Facebook: https://www.facebook.com/DannieFrenchCoach/

ELEVEN

Mirror Mirror, Looking Backward to See Forward

Kristine "Unique" McPeak

Looking in the rearview mirror, I never saw how dark my teenage thoughts were.

Noxious, like weeds growing by the side of the road, the ones you ignore while traveling, my thoughts grew more insidious each day as they cast their mighty shadows. I was learning how to drive, yet, I could not see my own blind spots: My thoughts.

These invasive thought patterns were as real as the potholes and pitfalls in the road. And they severely damaged my steering, nearly causing me to veer off course permanently. I was no stranger to suicidal thoughts at 15 years of age, and during COVID with 52 trips under my seatbelt.

Awkward, pimply, and insecure, I was never confident in my navigational skills. Neither driving, nor as an adult. Isolated and lonely, disoriented, and astray, I definitely didn't have any resources. No GPS to guide me out of my gloom. Never being taught to regulate my emotions, I was either explosive or silently imploding. There was no neutral.

My parents tried steering me down different roads. I was grounded for the better part of my sophomore year because my best friend and I found trouble at every turn. I didn't even confide in her.

She never knew the depths of my darkest thoughts, and my parents were just as unaware. After she moved away, I spiraled quickly, feeling utterly alone. I no longer had anyone riding shotgun.

My Dad taught me to spend more time looking through the windshield than getting caught up in what was behind me. Many of my life lessons were taught while riding shotgun as my Dad drove carpool. He said we were the ones who "installed our buttons." And, we could "choose to not let them get pushed." We "could uninstall them."

It would take decades before his wisdom made *any* sense. It would prove invaluable, returning back to me tenfold during COVID. On the way to junior high, he made up silly words to songs on the radio, singing to cajole me out of my sullen moods. It never worked. I grew even more angry. I wanted to laugh with him, but I stopped myself. And, while my friends were in the backseat swooning over my Dad's charm and charisma, nobody knew I was silently seething with self-hatred.

My secrets were well hidden. We are only as sick as our secrets. Being vulnerable about my suffering was not in my wheelhouse. My parents would have listened and sought help. I often found myself silently counting to 10 before I would say anything difficult. The words rarely came. I would recount, and still no words. My tongue was tied in frustrating knots, and I couldn't find a way to express my darkest fears.

I constantly recycled thoughts. One of the darkest ones had me questioning if I had never been born, would my family have been better off without me? Trapped by my blind spots, it was turbulent behind my secrets and my pretend smiles. I didn't know my inner suffering could affect my physical health or that my mental turmoil could affect my body.

I did know that I needed to shi(F)t gears, but I just didn't know how. My dad would fine me .25 every time I swore. "Shi(F)t" is my fun way of swearing without swearing. Shi(F)ting life's sh*t. The (F) used to stand for a word far different than "Fun."

Foolishly, I thought fueling my teenage mind and mood with alcohol and amphetamines would help me "fit in," and that marijuana, LSD or cocaine were ways out of this darkness. That numbing myself would help me feel better, or at least, less miserable. I was spinning my wheels and couldn't see my value or my worth.

If I could reverse time, I would have listened to my parents' guidance and followed their road map for me. I would have laughed more at my Dad's silly songs, especially knowing how brain chemistry and inner dialogue can be profoundly altered. Unfortunately, due to the nature of our teen years, we give our peers' opinions far more importance than the wisdom and support of our parents or elders.

I never did feel any happier when I was altering my moods. I did artificially "fit in." However, I didn't feel any less alone and could see no other route. I was self-destructive and on the partying path, avoiding dark emotions: Hoping they would disappear, or that I could disappear.

For decades, I carried my shame, secrets and shadows along with unhealthy coping tools. They'd become a heavy burden. I grew adept at stuffing and hiding my feelings that festered beneath the surface, impacting all of my relationships. They were waiting to be healed and cleared in my 50's, during a pandemic.

If I could go back to the future, I'd introduce my teenage self to Emotional Freedom Technique and the calming capacity of breathing mindfully. I would've learned all of the other tools that I thankfully rediscovered during those dark and dreary COVID cave days. I felt alone and even more despondent than in my turbulent teens.

Six months before COVID contained us in our homes, I had left a domestic violent relationship. Some of my familial relationships were strained. I hadn't spoken to my only sibling for three years. Deep down, I knew that I was heading full speed towards a cliff. Numbing out, again, had me thinking that things would get better. The course I was on became darker and heavier with my avoidant behaviors and my unhealthy patterns.

I had the cruise control set to self-destruct. And I was beginning to not care. Until one desperate COVID day, I had nearly forgotten about these tools during the collective quarantine; those that I'd used personally and had begun teaching my Healing Touch clients. It was as if I had amnesia to these strategies I had been studying for ten years, self-regulating tools that are mostly absent in school. They certainly were not taught while I was in school or in college while earning an education degree.

During the pandemic, I was over-medicating. I was zoning out on movies, marijuana, alcohol, and ice cream. I craved connection, yet was abrasive in my conversations. I was getting lost in my secrets and shadows and grew more despondent. Distracting myself from doing the shadow work, I was losing myself in my addictions. My shadows became familiar, like old high school friends.

After yet another same old, same old, repetitive COVID day, one too many wine coolers, paired with the general 2020 vibes, my thoughts led to an especially dark place. I found myself in depressing daydreams of my story ending with mice chewing through wires, causing an electrical fire.

I could be one more COVID casualty and began entertaining suicidal thoughts on that random pandemic day. As a teenager, I vowed to not put my grandmother, Faith, through the loss of suicide. I wouldn't put my mother through that loss. My fur baby, Mr Lucky Kat Tales, shook me into the present. I couldn't abandon him during the pandemic and began to shi(F)t my thinking.

I had tools that I didn't have as a teenager. I knew how to shi(F)t perspective with Emotional Freedom Technique (EFT), and I could re-write my narrative using Rapid Resolution Therapy. I now had road maps or tools to lead me through the darkness. I started tapping, gently tapping on my collarbones, while speaking my secrets and shadows aloud.

Tapping about sibling estrangement. Tapping around lifelong friendships turned sour. Tapping around my strained communication with friends. EFT tapping saved my life more than once while I was in that domestic violence household, and it would save me once more.

As those shadows reared their ugly heads during COVID, I began addressing them. I couldn't avoid them. During quarantine, I learned to embrace some of my more familiar shadows: conflict, inadequacy, intolerance, stress, my propensity for distractions, and feelings of mediocrity, to name a few.

I revisited my EFT studies with women from all over the world on Zoom calls, slowly forming other connections by showing up. I was becoming part of a Gene Keys online community, connecting with people who contemplated deep spiritual concepts. We discussed shadows, gifts or ways out of the shadows, and higher frequencies or Siddhis: Bliss, Peace, and Forgiveness.

Zoom helped me find a place where I "fit in." Or rather, "fit out," beginning to embrace the sides of myself that I kept hidden as a teenager. The "not normal" sides.

With so much COVID time on my hands, I began diving even deeper into another course of study: Rapid Resolution Therapy. Meeting more people around the world who were focusing on becoming free and clear, slowly, I began to feel even more connected. Alive. Vibrant. Vital. Less alone. I began to embrace myself and my shadows during a time when we could not embrace one another.

I began to crave clarity, taking a hard look at my alcohol and marijuana addictions. Until then, I'd only briefly *considered* sobriety in my late 40s when I met a man struggling with alcoholism: a man struggling with his own anger issues. The man who nearly strangled me one year before COVID.

With three years of sobriety, I've never felt clearer. I no longer distract myself from life's twists. I feel my feelings, such as anger, move through it and then take healthy steps. I now teach women how to transform their anger. It's been a bumpy ride, and one I wouldn't trade for anything.

Imagine you are driving an old rusty car. Your gas tank reads empty and you have no map or compass. Not a clue where you are or which way to turn. And your cell phone is dead. Did I also mention it's a new moon, and the middle of the night?

You don't have to go through this alone. That is how I felt most of my life. The roads I traveled have prepared me to be your passenger.

I'll help you see the sunflowers, not the weeds, by the side of the road. As my Dad reminded my sister and I while bursting through clouds in his tiny airplane, the "sun is always shining, somewhere, even if we cannot see it." I can be your co-pilot. I can help you formulate and navigate a new map. Help you unplug your "buttons."

If you're feeling any of this, I share my story so you know you're not alone. There is a light at the end of the tunnel. No matter how far you've already traveled, it's never too late to change the road you're on.

No matter your age, there are countless paths to different destinations. To transformation. To inner peace. To bliss. I could be your guide. We can navigate the shadows together.

We can have up to 30,000 thoughts a day. Until COVID, I focused too heavily on the negative ones. For most of my journey, I was afraid to look forward and hesitant to look in the rearview mirror at my patterns of self-induced suffering.

Even equipped with these tools, there were still so many things that I didn't want to see about myself. Just looking into the mirror was difficult. Painful at times. During one particularly difficult period in my life, prior to the pandemic, while in that domestic violent physically abusive relationship, I covered all of my mirrors with scarves, not wanting to see my reflection.

I didn't like catching glimpses of myself in the rearview mirror.

And, in 2020 I had a boudoir photo shoot and was told to look into a mirror and talk to myself. My initial thoughts were not uplifting, and my face reflected those thoughts. Then, a phrase came to me, "You don't have to take anyone's shi(F)t, including your own." As I chuckled to myself, she took the photo.

When I look into the mirror now, and my internal dialogue doesn't reflect positively, I start tapping, EFT style. This tool is a great tune-up, powerful like jumper cables, giving me a fresh new perspective.

The gold, the alchemical shi(F)ts, the gifts that came from my COVID cave were learning that I could transform the shadows. I am becoming a different mentor and healer, helping people reconstruct their lives at their pace. Some people never start their transformative journey, stuck in fear at the starting line.

So, I have learned to wait for clients who resonate with my story and my teachings. With their permission or an invitation, I can be their mirror, helping them see their non-productive patterns. I customize tools and strategies to help you feel better, making your shadows easier to see and easier to shi(F)t.

I no longer worry about "fitting in;" rather, I prefer to "fit out." I'm now comfortable gazing into my mirror, recording my voice, making videos, showing up, and being seen. While finding my own way out of my darkness, I can now better serve you in facing your darkest fears. Together, we move towards finding your own inner strength to experience freedom.

If you're a woman needing to shi(F)t self-degrading thoughts or release trauma, I can support and be your guide. If you are focusing on overcoming addictions or taming your anger, I can help you to uncover, notice and then shi(F)t the hidden aspects that hold you back.

Together, we can transform the darkness. We find the gifts in the shadows. We transmute, we alter, we alchemize. We shatter beliefs that no longer serve us individually or collectively. I could guide you gently down new pathways, helping you to rewire and re-write your stories and patterns, leading to inner liberation and finding freedom from self-destructive thoughts, habits or disorders.

Once you've learned ways to regulate your nervous system, we dive into a modified tool that I embraced while completing my health coaching program. We look at "primary foods," not what we ingest, but rather areas in which we may be out of balance. We assess to help prioritize your energy and actions.

I am the familiar friend who rides in your passenger seat. The friend that I wish I had all those years ago. I help you stay confident and alert on unfamiliar roads. I remind you to rest before you crash. I help you discover your blind spots and keep your eyes on the road.

Every new choice in life can lead to new consequences. Every turn can take us in new directions, to a different destination. I can assist you in charting a new course. Spotting the signposts and markers that you are on the right path.

As I've learned to shi(F)t my shadows, I can teach you how to navigate yours. We transform and alchemize together. I reflect for you how your transformation can look and feel. We can no longer be afraid of being lost in the dark. As I heal, you heal. We all heal.

You are me, and I am you. We are beautiful reflections of one another. Look ahead, and only glance in your rearview mirror occasionally. Buckle up, the ride may be bumpy, and you are not alone.

Activities

What drives you? Are you stuck in reverse or neutral? What keeps you from moving forward? Where are you spinning your wheels?

Here are some activities that have helped me shi(F)t through my darkness. These practices can help you become more aware of your non-productive thoughts that don't promote a sense of empowerment. I've been practicing the following phrase for decades, and it helps me start turning my thoughts around quickly.

1. When you notice your thinking is stuck in reverse, say this disruptor out loud:
"Cancel, Clear, Delete, Replace"
Then shi(F)t your inner dialogue, replacing it with a new narrative:
From "I can't" to "I know I can."
From "It's hard" to "It's easy."
From "I'm afraid" to "I lean into my fears."
From "I don't know how" to "I'll figure it out."
See how shi(F)ting perspective can start to uplift your mood.

2. I love breathing techniques as a fast way to activate the Parasympathetic Nervous System. By practicing these on a regular basis, when you *need* self-regulation, they are much easier to draw upon. Notice how you feel this very moment and try one of these breathing techniques. If you don't notice a shi(F)t, repeat for a few minutes, or try another one.

Left Nostril - When you need to put on the brakes, breathe in and out of your left nostril.
Right Nostril - When you need extra gas, breathe in and out of your right nostril.

4444 - Inhale for the count of 4, hold for the count of 4, exhale for 4, hold for 4, and repeat.

Pursed Lip - Inhale through your nose as if smelling a flower. Exhale slowly and gently through your lips as if blowing at a candle to flicker, but not blow out, and repeat. Try to make the exhalation twice as long as the inhalation.

3. This next technique I use when I have a strong emotional reaction, am triggered or notice the darker thoughts that I would have kept to myself and dared not say out loud. You know, the ones you don't tell your best friend or the ones you would never say out loud to an innocent child. This is when I start tapping.

In the past, I might have completed the following sentence with the word, "ugly" or "miserable" or "worthless." This Emotional Freedom Technique (EFT) tapping exercise is a regular self-care practice for me:

"Even though right now, I feel _____, I can learn to be OK with this situation"
Or

"I can learn to be OK with _not_ being OK with this situation"

While saying the sentence three times, gently rub or tap underneath your collarbones. This technique has more to it, and I highly recommend you book a 1:1 session with me or another EFT Practitioner to help you navigate the ins and outs of learning this self-regulating technique.

EFT helps to release hidden self-destructive thought patterns that rob us of joy, and EFT also releases tension and stress from our body.

Which one was your favorite? Do you feel different? Can you practice mindful breathing whenever you check your phone for messages or the time? When can you add this new practice to your day?

We don't learn to drive our first time behind the wheel. Developing skills takes practice and an expert guide. Are you ready to shi(F)t gears and form new beliefs? I am ready to be your guide!

Kristine "Unique" McPeak

Kristine McPeak is a lifestyle mentor and is already an International Best-Selling author in the book, *Entangled No More*.

In 1992, Kristine earned her BS in Elementary Education. Never landing a formal classroom, life became her teacher. She then became a Certified Laughter Leader and began leading therapeutic laughter groups, sharing the health benefits with businesses.

Earning a Physical Therapist Assistant degree in 2012, she went on to study Healing Touch, a continuing education program for nurses. She is trained as a Level 4 Practitioner.

When a crisis arose, Kristine learned about Emotional Freedom Technique (EFT). Having experienced the effectiveness, she studied to become an EFT Practitioner, sharing this tool with her clients.

In 2019, she furthered her mind-body-spirit knowledge through the Institute for Integrative Nutrition, becoming a Health Coach, and has been a student of Rapid Resolution Therapy since 2021. She plans to study in the fall of 2024 to become a Gene Keys Guide.

Continuing to develop these new skills to help others reframe, shi(F)t and release unbeneficial core beliefs, she now helps others become free and clear from lifelong struggles.

Follow her personal FaceBook page, to learn how you can join her monthly Zoom classes, on the first Friday, (f)ART-ing Around with Friends. There, you will be encouraged to use art in safe and playful ways, as you are gently guided to notice your inner critic. Her 2nd Saturday Series are classes that offer practical tools in a fun setting.

In the meantime, if you need to quiet your inner critic, or are feeling stuck, reach out to her at kristinemcpeak@gmail.com, join her private Facebook Group, Play in the Quantum with Kristine, or book a session at https://pensight.com/x/kristineuniquemcpeak

Keep tuned in for Kristine's ageless allegories for kiddos of all ages, as The Adventures of Mr Lucky Kat Tales debut in 2025.

TWELVE

the pearl in fire
Aleph Drasmin

rage…

from the tender age of 6 through my mid-twenties, my memories are mostly under a hazy all-consuming redness that also created disconnect and "loss" of memory. i did not know how to recognize, let alone avoid, being swept under the clear fog of rage until after entering my thirties. devotion to love and living the sacred way is the core through which i transform pain into gold, and remain the pillars between which i dance this messy beautyfull life.

rage is…
ultimately a mask for sadness
grief unfelt and often denied
until it rips flooding emotion

it wasn't until after my only brother, whom i also raised as a son, transitioned from the earth plane in 2021 that i faced the depths of the rage i had held within me. coupled with what seemed a rapid degeneration of my hands, a nuclear bomb erupted scarring more than i.

the volcanic matter was water, thick steaming heaviness in 2020 that was also the beginning of my initiation into death rite studies. for the past 5 years i had used a single word as the intention for the year ahead in lieu of lists and goals, and my word for that year was... trust.

i had known for nearly a decade, from a western-medical diagnosis, there was high probability my hands would cease to function by the time i hit my thirties. yet before that life-changing doctors' visit completed, i had made a decision to refuse this judgement upon my body. i chose instead to divert attention into disciplined daily self-care, and with it, unbeknownst to me then, initiation into shadow alchemy. first nutrition and physical fitness focused, alongside ongoing therapy to overcome the extensive traumas from childhood, then weaving in meditation and fasting, and over time plant medicine allies.

for a period of time, all seemed well. i could feel a trickling of weakening in the measure of strength i had in adolescence through adulthood, yet brushed it off as natural aging. until the smoke of the Pacific NorthWest fires of 2020 rolled in, and with it the tidal wave of rage.

it would take me over two years to process all that transpired that late summer leading into fall. then, barely 9 months into this initiation, amidst a full blown internal war with denial, my phone rang as i stood at my front door on the way to the passport office.

my entire world imploded. i already knew... and...

"doya's dead" no greeting...the first call and last call i ever received from mother...

"what" a strange flat response i observed, utterly detached and accepting...almost expectant.

the pearl in fire

"he's gone!" sobbed my mother through the whisper of a scream, speaking of brother-son.

i immediately got to setting up an altar for bardo, suddenly the downloads of the past 9 months as crystal clear as these words you now read. i had also received several gifts from the land and from new friends in the previous months, and in that moment innerstood how to use them – crystals, feathers, bones, incenses, tapestries, and other sacred tools to craft a ceremonial altar fit for a king. i covered my face in ashes, went to the store to buy black dye, and by dusk my white veils, shirts, soul, and heart were all one saturating in darkness.

i like to tell myself i held my external composure mostly well through the remaining year, even as internally i felt myself liquifying much like i perceive a caterpillar might feel molting in its cocoon. yet as the winter crept in and 13 moon cycles circuited since the smoky initiation, a pain erupted in the body unlike anything i had ever experienced before.

fire ants crawling inside my bones!
nerves coming online, screaming for space!

i was living with a friend, a past lover, a gift from god-goddess through the eruption of frothing rage and depths of spewing pain. he inbodied patience and showed me ways of love i had never known, yet too often was he also scarred by both my words and actions.

words and actions that did not reflect the love and gratitude I have for him, and yet the ultimately lifetimes of rage needing space to be seen-heard-felt, greater in the moment, sifted through.

quite literally space.

this is the first key i share with you and encourage- empower you to use through the uncovery of your own shadows and challenges, dear reader and fellow alchemist.

the shadow aspect of self, what one might consider undesirable-difficult-taboo, shows up as rage, denial, indifference, workaholism, addiction, codependency, hyper independence, people pleasing, ungrounded activated clairvoyant gifts, etc. the keys i share here are a few of many practices i continue to implement in my daily life, because the shadow exists with and for the light. i, and you, are the light and also the shadow, and learning how to dance with both is what my alchemy is all about.

as within so without , as above so below.
this is a saying i stumbled upon in a metaphysical book in my mid twenties. only a few years later, as the rage inside started seeping through, i finally understood how important having a clean and organized home is to overall thriving wellness. i asked the friend i lived with for a declutter and reset of our home to support both our sanities, yet ultimately was not met which further fueled the now sieve-like leaking of steamy venom.

the first key
declutter, darling!
get rid of all that is broken and torn, if it cannot be fixed or mended.
donate the excess, redistribute the wealth, make room for new.
new can also be the same "old" yet refreshed and upgraded.

in the past decade plus of consciously engaging rage, not always successfully yet gratefully more so since the arrival of my first white hair, our relationship has evolved to what is now one of peacefull acceptance and devotional tending.

denial is considered the first stage of grief, and acceptance the last.

yet in my experience, the stages of grief are akin to interchanging spokes of a wheel that move to the beat of wild untamable heart.

my acceptance of a need for external space to make room for the internal decluttering was denied, further fueling the rage that had my throbbing aching hands more than once meeting walls in a mad attempt to redirect the venom away from my dear friend. until i could no longer, and pain shattered through the hubris walls from inside which flooded sad.

so much sad…
…for the soft playfull joy of childhood never experienced
…for the absence of gentle and supportive love from parents
…for the thrust into adulthood at the age of 6 to raise a brother like a son
…for the desecration of innocence in that same year through the first forced participating and witness of what would be nearly a decade of cultist and satanic rituals
… for a youth and early adulthood of wasteful drinking and chemical drowning
… for years of pouring my love in countless ways into relationships that had not shown up in equivalence during my hours of need
… for careers that had fallen away and with it the friendships i had held so dear
… for the illusions i had clung to around experiencing family with my own blood family
… for hands that could no longer use my counting beads for, the daily breath and chanting practices i had consistently honoured for 7 years, anchoring my daily center
… for the decreased inability to show up for myself in all the needed and playfull ways
… for the inability to show love through acts of service and healing touch to this friend who had been both physically and financially supportive through my many waves
… for the understanding of the unseen worlds my clairvoyant gifts were aware of yet had still to discover forms of expression for

... for the years of masking my awesomeness and my challenges after years in childhood of any "abnormalities" whipped bloody out of me
... for the years of running, hiding, and denying my pain and grief at the threat of my brothers' life who now no longer lived
... for lifetimes of love hungered for and either unmet or abused in perversion and neglect
... for the silent little girl inside that is pure love expressed through poetry and laughter
... for the darkness i had yet to face and could no longer hide or deceive myself from
... oceans of sad!
mountains shedding...

the years of 2017 through 2023 were dark, waves of grief often bringing me to my knees gasping to god-goddess to hold me through. i did not start feeling the emotions on a visceral-cellular soul-ullar level till the winter of 2020, yet through the years i had been developing a daily practice that is now a part of the CPR deck i finally assembled and published in 2021 during the "numb from shock" phase of grief. this deck of cards, inspired by my own need for "how to feel my feelings and communicate my thoughts-needs-boundaries", is an A-Z guide in the form of 26 simple cards designed for all ages to cultivate emotional intelligence.

this is **the second key** i share with you, dear reader and fellow alchemist, the A-B-C harmony helpers.

upon rising before grabbing the phone or getting out of bed, do the following practice to softly shift from dreaming to waking and set a gentle empowered tone for the day ahead

A. Acknowledge self with gentle touch, one hand on heart and the other on the belly in full presence with the body

the pearl in fire

B. Breathe in
    A. Affirm in the pause " I woke up today"

B. Breathe out and

C. (feel the) Connect (between) mind (words) – heart (gentle awareness) - body (touch)

Repeat the above A-B-C steps for each of the following sentences...
" I woke up today.
I am in this body.
All I am is valid.
It is safe to be me.
I am loved and I am love."

the A-B-C harmony helpers is a simple yet powerful practice any being can initiate at any time. you are also welcome to revise my suggestion, and add affirmations and more as your roots strengthen.

the A-B-C harmony helpers is also a wonderful tool to use at any time throughout the day, to ground back into the body and recenter into the heart, or whenever a challenging emotion arises. it continues to personally help me avoid, or if unavoidable calm down an awetistic panic attack.

there are more steps for full emotional intelligence-body awareness, 26 total to be precise, and are available in the form of small square cards that can be used as an empowering and loving guide and game for all ages. yes, you guessed it! it is 'the CPR deck'!

yet the first three steps are enough, for here; and sometimes all one can do, especially after those triggers arise. way to GrOw!

the core key is consistent daily practice. i invite you to allow play and pleasure to be your motivation whenever resistance, aka growing edges, arise around showing up to your self-love practiced.

what started out as breath awareness and meditation practices for personal wellness in my mid twenties slowly evolved through my late twenties. my love for languages and need for empowered awetistic friendly tools, in addition to the years of academia and spiritual study, wove themselves with the innate wisdom i had tapped into through my "healing" journey and in divine time revealed soul-nourishing love-empowering gifts under liquified denial.

you may have noticed dear reader the way i have chosen to share my story contains unique words, different spelling, and intriguing punctuation. this is all intentional, because our language – or rather the words we use and how – creates the very moment existing in this present.

even after the waves of sad poured through, sometimes in soft trickles and sometimes in tempestuous avalanches, there was still a lot of energy needing a vehicle for expression.

as i disciplined in my personal practices, deepening the balance between physical self-care and spiritual devotion-growth, rage showed me how to harness its energy into constructive and creative forms…
- the anchoring of my legacy
- the straightening of my spine
- the regeneration of my hands
- the cleansing from multigenerational trauma
- the purification from multidimensional karma
- the creation and publication of the CPR deck
- the opening of my gallery
- the channeling and publication of my first book
- this sharing here in my 2nd book and 1st co-authored book

the more i accept myself for who i am, a spirit in a temporary body with all the humanness of being a highly sensitive neurodivergent on the awetism spectrum and with an incredible amount of scar tissue plus the daily challenges the current regeneration of my hands bring, the emotional waters within me remain calm most days. and when the waters get choppy, there are simply tools such as the keys shared here to easefully ride the waves.

master key… daily practice
    the A-B-C harmony helpers
    a clean organized home
    the entire CPR deck
    breathe, feel, be
    breathe, be
    breathe
    breathe
    breathe

as i strengthened within, i learned how to befriend my emotions. as my allies, they continue to guide me into deeper innerstanding of and love for self. to innerstand means to have an integrated understanding of self, that comes through and includes daily supportive and nourishing internal and external practices.

over time, through the discovery of how to love all of myself, the attention shifted from sad to witness. here in the seat of witness i learnt to recognize the red haze of rage that sometimes is rightful rage, and sometimes is a veil for a crossed boundary or an unacknowledged emotion. this understanding triggered a deep inner child and teenager decluttering and reunion with the heart, which with the practice of forgiveness and actionable accountability led to the inbodyment of a thriving empowered adult.

ultimately all the experiences of my many lives molded me into the woman i am today, inspired the legacy i am proud to have founded, and continue to fuel the creation of art, poetry, stories, songs, and self-guided empowering content for all beings to use with their own free will so as to also thrive in the being human experience.

the path and process of and from acknowledging to accepting a shadow can be a lifetime adventure, and does get easier over time. with gentle daily tending, the illusionary walls within soften to reveal a heart of divinity and pearls of gold.

Aleph Drasmin

Alchemist, Artist, Author – Aleph Drasmin is a tea-drinking earth-worshipping prayerform dancer who dreams alive words in various creative forms such as story, poetry, song, and more. She is also the founder of Drasmin DreamWorks, a higher education eco-centric foundation devoted to bridging science, spirit, and love. Some of her creative works include a 10 year collection of vision inspired paintings and spiritual poetry art, the CPR deck - an A-Z guide in the form of 26 simple cards designed for all ages to cultivate emotional intelligence, I AM - a meditation poetry collection, and an ever-growing library of self-guided downloadable content to empower thriving (as a highly sensitive neurodivergent) in the being human experience. She is a well-known host of tea parties and wombman temple circles, her favourite ways to play are through drumming, hugging and kissing trees, and slaying at scrabble, and her go to plant allies include blue lotus, datura, and cannabliss.

Connect with and explore more at https://linktr.ee/drasmindreamworks

THIRTEEN

How Art Caused Me to Face the Shadow of Perfectionism

Ikenna Lughna

According to the authority figures in my life, high school was the time to prepare for and find the perfect college with the perfect degree to land you the perfect job.

Perfection became my armor, allowing me to survive the standards of American public education. I completely bought into the idea that perfection was the ultimate goal to everything. Any feedback people gave me that made me feel like my choices weren't already perfect caused me to immediately ditch the idea and go back to the drawing board.

I was the person who did the whole group project in middle school. My classmates usually didn't complain. They'd need to do one thing here or there, and then I'd spend my whole weekend perfecting the project. My mom told me recently that teachers were surprised by what I believed they expected in terms of the intricacy of the projects they assigned me.

During that time, I thought perfectionism was a trait to put on resumés. It was a source of pride. Perfectionism did its job to some degree. I was able to get things done on a pretty high level. It would cause me to practice certain skills until I felt I mastered them to my standards. However, I was completely unaware of the ever-growing shadow behind me as time went on.

The general layman considers perfectionism to be only a positive term. It helps people have higher standards and drive to meet goals. Sure. That's one side. However, most of us perfectionists who leave the shadow side unchecked will run into the walls of burnout, avoidance, and low distress tolerance. These symptoms may sound similar to generalized anxiety, and that's because perfectionism's shadow fuels anxiety's shadow.

But wait. Isn't anxiety ALL shadow? Those of us struggling with anxiety could place it in the overall category of "bad," but we're just so deep in the shadow, we don't realize that anxiety initially served us as well! Anxiety in controlled doses can motivate us to do things. In overwhelming doses, it can paralyze us. Perfectionism can team up with this anxiety shadow.

What does that mean?

• You may spiral if you make (or you perceive that you make) a social faux pas. "I wasn't perfect in this social interaction."

• You may crawl out of your skin when someone offers feedback on anything you're doing. "I'm not being a perfect parent, sibling, spouse, employee, writer, artist, musician, athlete, etc."

• You may compare your current progress to someone else you believe has "made it." "I'm unhappy because I'm not where they're at. I'm unhappy because I suck at this. This is too hard. I'm just always going to be bad at this."

• You may constantly daydream and love making to-do lists but are paralyzed about doing the tasks. "I have to do this entire task in one take. Before I do this task, I have to make sure everything is set up perfectly for me to feel at peace doing the task."

I could write a whole book giving examples of perfectionistic ideals, but these are a few to get you started in realizing just how pervasive perfectionism could be in your life.

Burnout

But how did we get to this point?

There was a malfunction in the proverbial perfectionism factory, and the alarm bells didn't seem to go off until the whole operation had to shut down. Perfectionism is about results. To continue the factory metaphor, management only cared about the numbers, not employee health. Overworked and underpaid, mistakes were made under the radar, one thing led to the other, and catastrophe fell upon the company.

Welcome to burnout.

This metaphor may feel strangely realistic to the world's workforce. That's because it is. Much of society is covered by the darkness of perfection's shadow. Sacrificial service is praised. Boundaries are punished. This is all for the sake of reaching the ever-rising standards each day. This societal shadow seeps into our souls if we're not conscious of it.

I want to soothe your perfectionism at this moment because it may feel VERY called out. Or it may feel self-critical that it wasn't perfect in being conscious of the societal shadow until now. Ever feel like hindsight is the ultimate slap in the face? Perfectionism can use hindsight to fuel self-criticism. Even though logically we know that we couldn't technically know everything we know now, perfectionism holds the new knowledge in front of us and says, "See? If only you knew this back then, and you wouldn't have made this grave error."

These thoughts can become so overwhelming that we can burn out. Originally, perfectionism may have gotten you out of bed and working on projects to reach desired results. But now, it feels like someone not listening to your inner needs. "A sick day? That doesn't stop a lot of people. You're going to fall behind!" Comparing. Criticizing. Over and over and over.

This cycle runs us into the ground. We become desperate, hopeless, and exhausted. Then, we wake up a little. "Oh. I haven't been listening to my body. Time to learn how to set boundaries."

This is where low distress tolerance comes in.

Distress Tolerance

When you think about being uncomfortable, what comes up for you? Do you sit in your discomfort? Flee it? Freeze? Barrel blindly forward?

Our window of distress tolerance determines how much peace, self-awareness, and decision-making ability we can maintain when in the face of discomfort.

When we realize we've let perfectionism manage the factory, we also see there were no systems in place to warn us when we go overboard. Alternatively, perfectionism would use those warning signs as badges of honor. "You're sore and exhausted? That's proof of a good day's work!" When burnout hits, we promise ourselves not to reach that point ever again. But that itch to reach "the standard" and get back on track while attempting to recover is basically a limbo level in Dante's Inferno.

You just want to relax but don't know how to. Perfectionism creeps in to remind you that you need to constantly be doing or else you're failing. And guess what? If we don't have distress tolerance, we certainly have no distress tolerance for failure. We also don't have distress tolerance for putting in effort. Trying leads to comparison to the standard, which leads to self-criticism, which leads to exhaustion. Rinse and repeat.

So we say "NO MORE!" in the midst of burnout. If you can't even dream of doing this, you may still be stuck in earlier stages of the burnout cycle. However, there are many of us who have put our foot down to the extreme. This is where we go into the metaphorical factory, install every alarm system, and crank them to the highest level of sensitivity. Then, the alarms go off every 20 seconds, which makes it impossible to do anything. Each emergency protocol is exhausting when you have to do it 50 times a day.

May as well abandon the factory. That'll feel better, right?

Avoidance

This is where our low distress tolerance takes every little feeling of discomfort and considers it a red flag. We can feel uncomfortable doing any task, so we put it off. We can feel uncomfortable not understanding how to play a game that friends are teaching us, so we say we won't play. We avoid social interactions knowing we will feel uncomfortable navigating those spaces. We avoid trying different creative endeavors because the learning process is uncomfortable.

Comparison still exists. The desire to connect with others still exists. Welcome to another level of hell where we struggle between the fear of missing out and avoiding the immense discomfort that comes with making sure the interaction is perfect (which leads to scrutinizing every aspect of the interaction).

While we go inward to try and escape perfectionistic self-criticism, it will follow us to the deepest depths of our being. We keep running from it because it's so enormous now, and we're terrified to turn around and face it.

Art

I started to face my perfectionist shadow when I discovered a practice called Neurographica. It's a technique that Russian psychologist and professor, Pavel Piskarev, developed. He created a training institute that teaches this practice at all levels.

Neurographica consists of an eight-step system where you think of a topic intellectually and then use specific art techniques to process the sensations that come up. The first few times that I did it,

I *hated* the discomfort that came up. That's one of the beautiful things about this practice.

After deciding the topic, there's a step where you place the tension on the page in what I like to call a "scribble scream." Neurographica calls it "composition" or "catharsis." The scribble scream is the egoic shit we thought about expressed through scribbling on the page for about two to three seconds. This was my favorite part of the process initially. You don't know what you're going to get! I would avoid art because I would have an expectation in mind, but wouldn't know how to get the blank canvas to the final product. Starting with a scribble gave me something to work with. It forced me to simply sit in each step of the journey instead of worrying about it compared to my expected destination.

The next step is one that weaves throughout the rest of the practice. Neurographica coins the term "conjoining" to round and smooth out all of the sharpness of the scribble. The sharp angles can be from the line itself and from the intersections the scribble creates. This used to be the step I despised. This step takes time and effort. You're forced to examine the scribble and be willing to see the intersections. Our avoidance of discomfort can become so strong that we can feel like we're rehabilitating an atrophied muscle when relearning to recognize and take care of the sharp corners. Perfectionism may step in to criticize you throughout this process as well. "That doesn't look right. This is too much work. What's the point of this? I don't see or feel the results that I want. Wow, look how good the instructor's example is. You suck."

The next steps involve Neurographic Lines, shapes, colors, and more rounding. The specific "Neurographic Line" is a technique where you consciously make lines that may not follow the original desires your brain has in mind. Your hand wants to move the marker up? Challenge it and go left. It wants to continue to go left? Go down. This practice alone made me curious about my brain's habits and patterns.

Neurographic lines connect the egoic catharsis to the edges of the page. This makes more intersections and sharpness but connects our egoic issue to the rest of the community. Our internal conflicts have ripple effects. The effects are different, but still happen, whether it's conflict from showing up or conflict from not showing up.

Once the Neurographic Lines are rounded, coloring or as Neurographica calls it, "archetyping," takes place. This still causes me discomfort at times. How many colors? Are the shapes I'm making pleasing to the eye? What colors look good? This step can make me want to avoid the discomfort and step away from the project altogether. It's good to notice sensations and thoughts like these that can come up in each step. Thankfully coloring a project that's simply for your own processing is a discomfort that's much smaller than other tasks your perfectionism has a chokehold around. And it's okay if this coloring discomfort feels gargantuan! You're still doing the work by facing it and reflecting on it.

The rest of the process involves more Neurographic Lines and rounding sharpness and intersections that come up. By the time I hit this point, a lot of the tension from the topic I scribble screamed about has fallen away. I can feel tired, but also with the tired I feel relief.

If you feel like the concept of "feeling your feelings" is too nebulous? Neurographica is an incredible way to feel like you're actually doing that. Perfectionism makes us avoid uncertainty. Uncomfortable feelings feel uncertain. Mindless scrolling, multiple pieces of media playing at once, binge eating, and substance use are a few examples of avoiding discomfort. Why is self-care like showering, tidying, hobbies, or movement so hard to do? Because our distress tolerance is nonexistent and sitting in the discomfort of doing any of those things is too overwhelming.

Neurographica and other experiential therapies show that through the processing of discomfort, we take care of ourselves. We can sit through the discomfort of showering and then feel better afterward, for example. We build ourselves up over time. Just like the perfectionism shadow snowballing into an immovable glacier of burnout, low distress tolerance, and avoidance, we can slowly pick ourselves back up and get back to enjoying ourselves in the journeys of different challenges.

How Art Caused Me to Face the Shadow of Perfectionism

Perfectionism scoffs at the "little steps" it takes to move through this shadow. Exploring art as a tool to navigate discomfort allows us to turn around and hold the part of us that believes perfectionism is the ultimate way to live. If the prospect of facing your shadows using art intrigues you, art therapy may be a great tool for you. I'd be honored to guide you through this process in the future.

Art has changed my life and helped me navigate my shadows with more curiosity and compassion. In the following practice, I'll lead you through some of the initial techniques that began to free me from my perfectionism.

Follow along to explore some techniques to bring art into processing and catharsis.

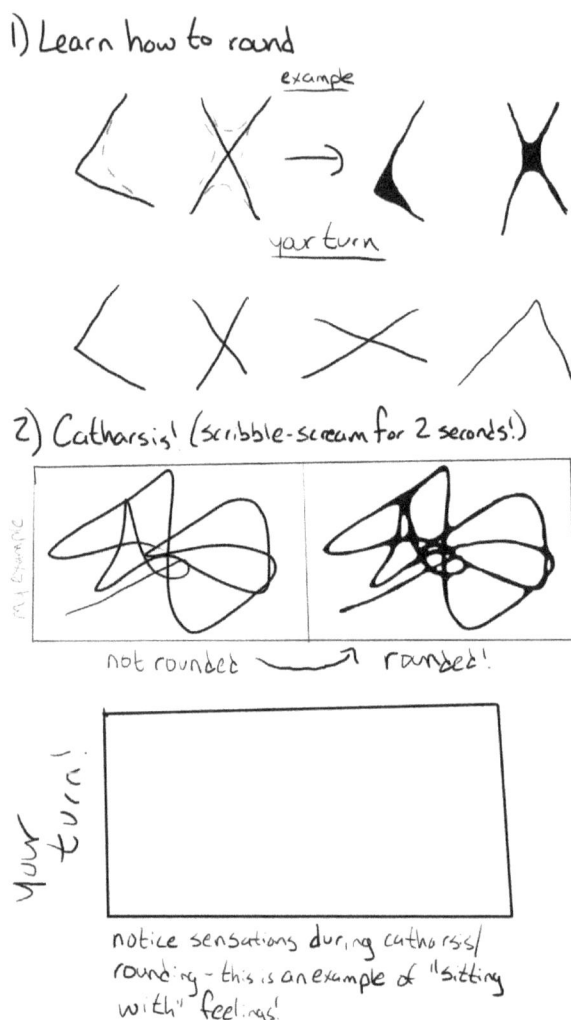

Ikenna Lughna

Ikenna Lughna, LGPC, MS, is a therapist specializing in helping queer and neurodivergent clients process their shadows. Even though eternally curious, Ikenna avoided the scary unknown of their shadows for many years. They're now diving into the inky blackness of discomfort more and showing others that they can do the same, even if these experiences can be immensely challenging.

As a creative, Ikenna enjoys making music and art and exploring the written word. They are an international best-selling author featured in the books *Rebel With A Cause: Being Different Doesn't Mean Being Less*, and *Raising Wild Ones: Empowering the Next Generation of Sovereign Leaders*.

Ultimately, Ikenna considers themselves a 'silly little guy,' and enjoys finding the awe and wonder in life.

Find out more about Ikenna and their different projects and communities at: https://linktr.ee/ikennagray

FOURTEEN

Light Mastery

Jessica Louise (Beal)

Darkness and the expanse make up the greatest portion of the universe. We cannot shy away from it. Through my studies of human behavior, consciousness, sound resonance and channeled wisdom, I think I have discovered the foundational pieces and framework that could allow us to alchemize suffering and move into a new way of being as a society: One where equality is created through creativity, generosity, arts, and community.

Four years ago, life changed quite substantially for me. I wrote about this account in my first collaborative project *Entangled No More*: *Women who broke free from toxic abuse and are now building empires*. Since that book, I have become better equipped to transmute energies and believe even more deeply that others can use this information to transmute and integrate their shadow.

So first, what is integration? Integration is the process we go through on a soul level each time we reach new information. As we integrate, we move through new levels of growth and achievement. This allows us to begin to manifest through aligning our passions with our purpose, instead of chasing desire through lust or comparison.

In Diagram 1, I share my theory on the sacred geometric code of a being in relation to its frequency when it is in alignment. This trinity consists of three aspects that make up the identity code: the Ego, the Self, and the little voice of God. Ascension and positive manifestation happen when the trinity moves through integrations on a cell and soul level. Information (consciousness) has a trinity of Discover, Understand, and Become. Together, they create a frequency that we could imagine looks like a Merkaba. The balance of these trinities will determine how quickly a soul moves from the discovery of new information to the becoming. Having the data downloaded allows the person to move to the next level of ascension on the path toward total enlightenment. Each level of ascension gets progressively easier until you have achieved the ultimate activation of the rainbow light body. At that time, you drop the body and return to the source. As seen in Diagram 2.

So let's back up. What is causing the current state of human suffering as a collective and what can we do to transmute it? Until this timeline, suffering and trauma were the only things that typically opened a human up to higher states of consciousness unless they used plant medicines and shamanic journeys. Fast forward to 2020; the entire earth's magnetic system shifted and this wave was felt GLOBALLY. Some souls couldn't calibrate to the frequency and intensity of the codes entering at that time, and because of this, we saw a high increase in suicide and drug-related deaths as they returned to source. They were checking out.

Through my own transmutation of suffering, I found synchronicities in my clients' stories over the past four years. It is clear we operate from the ego and the self out of safety and survival. This is especially true for women. This has caused a huge financial divide for our society as we navigate beliefs and codes around wealth, abundance, and success, particularly how much value we place on it and how we measure it.

I believe the root cause of this is directly related to generational childhood poverty trauma, as well as imbalanced DNA coding on an energetic level.

As a collective, this data has been handed down on a subconscious level through the wombs of women. I believe what epigenetics is showing us about the creation of the fetus in relation to when the reproductive organs and eggs are formed within that fetus. It is in fact at the time that the fetus is formed within the grandmother's womb. So what are these codes?

These codes manifest from situations of:

- Instability of finances
- Emotional neglect
- Physical neglect
- Sexual abuse
- Housing Insecurity
- Food insecurity
- Lack of access to quality foods, healthcare, education
- Childhood illness
- Vaccine injury
- Learning disabilities or mental illness in families
- Incest

Basically, any circumstance that may disrupt the natural wonder, curiosity, and safety of a child on any level, emotional or physical, can have a lasting effect on DNA generations down. At the root of that, we have a deeper coding: Shame. Beyond the shame, we have fear of death.

Because what do these things lead to? A shortened life span. This is the entrance to the unknown. Where will we end up without food, family, or protection? We fear being ostracized from the pack. It often feels like there is nothing beyond our current reality, especially when we release the identity of who we were told we are. Typically, all this happens before the age of 7, when our brain is not fully developed. However, the cells and DNA are recording codes.

What if we can become the witness and transmute this pain and trauma into power, recoding the system from the inside? How infinite is the expanse, and what if we had the ability to manifest from

THAT place? From the I AM instead of from an identity we didn't even write. Through using sound, light, video, and sharing our story with the world? Does that scare you?

When I launched my business, I could feel the pull on my soul, this was for me. I knew I felt a pull to this work, but I had no idea how I was going to make an impact. I began to dabble and play with the shadow online. I started to share my own story of what was working for me and how I was getting results through meditation, mindfulness, breathwork, and developing daily rituals geared towards success. Now, I help other skilled pros and visionary leaders tap in, clear old coding and step into their highest timelines through the very codes shown in this chapter and throughout this book. You may be reading this and feeling inspired to take action. However, I did not wake up one day and decide I was going to become who I am. It was a gradual shedding of the woman I thought I was and a continuous progression into the woman I wanted to become.

So we discovered the what, where, how, and why. What is the next step?

I believe the answer truly is in our personal and financial sovereignty. It is in the ways we don't show up or speak up for ourselves. In this way, we dismiss our desires because we are told they are vain, selfish, and greedy. I am dreaming of a world where equality is created through creativity, expressing your gifts and being monetized generously for them, generosity in information and giving back, arts, and community where we all can thrive, and I believe the time is now! It is within our power to release the codes to childhood poverty, to do the things we were told were silly or unimportant in the world. To step into the role of becoming the 3% who moves the needle forward.

What are you good at? What comes easily to you but maybe not others? What can you talk about for hours and not get bored or run out of ideas about? This is the first light code I guide clients to tap into. This alone is so potent.

Do you currently have the time to invest in doing this thing full-time? Would you like to? Would you like to be paid simply for existing?

If the answer is yes, I suggest you consider hitting play and starting to make short videos, providing value and insight on your topic. This will call in those who resonate and want to learn from you, or they will feel inspired to follow along.

Develop your message and create a $97 product that doesn't require you to trade time for money.

Build a community through using our most potent tool available to us: video. Research shows that only 3% of people will take action, create a lasting change and see a result. I believe if you are reading this book you are one of those 3%. You are here to weave your shadow with the person you truly came here to become. You are a beacon of light emerging from the globe. By calling back your own divine power and personal sovereignty, you create the perfect environment for healing and growth.

This is the path to freedom. To inner alchemy. The gap between the rich and the poor is only growing wider, which is why we need money in the hands of more visionaries, writers, artists and leaders. When we have more financial freedom, we can invest in better wellness, be active and contribute to our communities to do much more. Any time you catch yourself shrinking and playing small, go deeper, serve deeper, tap in.

Where can I be braver? How can this help someone else? What is the purpose of me experiencing this hardship?

Aligning your passion with your purpose creates the space for you to expand. Are you ready for it, 3%?

Diagram One:

Each time we reach new information, our consciousness goes through a sacred geometric pattern: Discover, Understand, Become; and, the trinity that makes up your being: Ego, Self, Little voice of God. The ego is not a bad thing; it is a form of us that creates and has personality. The importance is to have it in balance with everything else, and then move from that space with passion and purpose.

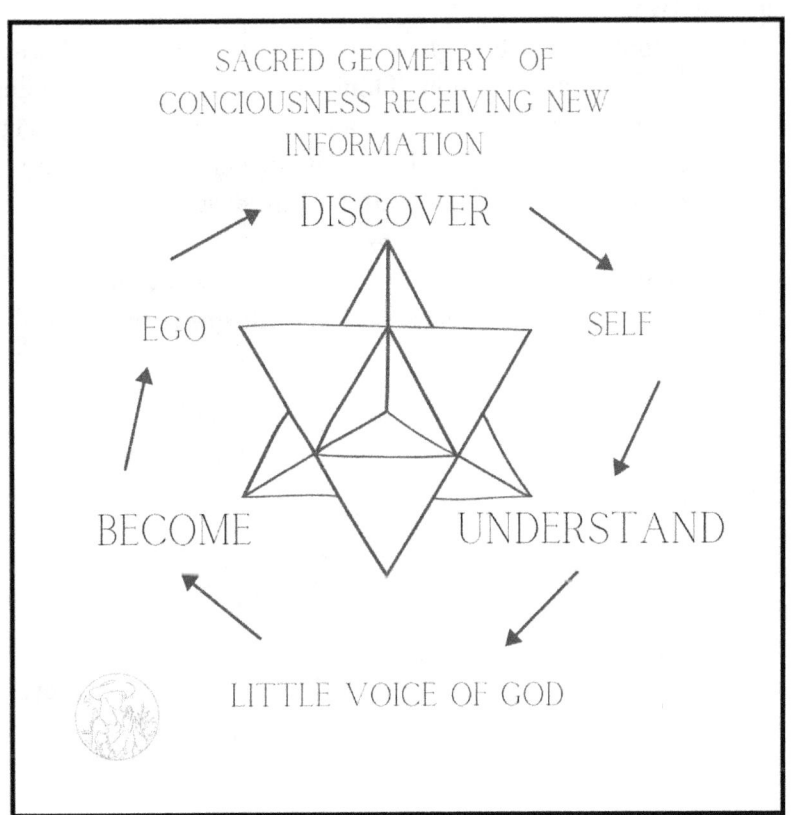

Diagram Two:

As our soul moves through integrations, it also moves through evolutionary levels of ascension. Think of these levels as a building. On the bottom floor you can hear traffic, smell trash on the streets, see a narrow view of the city, but what happens as we move up? The higher we go the less noise and unpleasantry, and the more we can see based on our perceptions. As you ascend, the external factors no longer play a role, and you are able to see your life's path and soul mission more clearly as you integrate through life's challenges.

Light Mastery

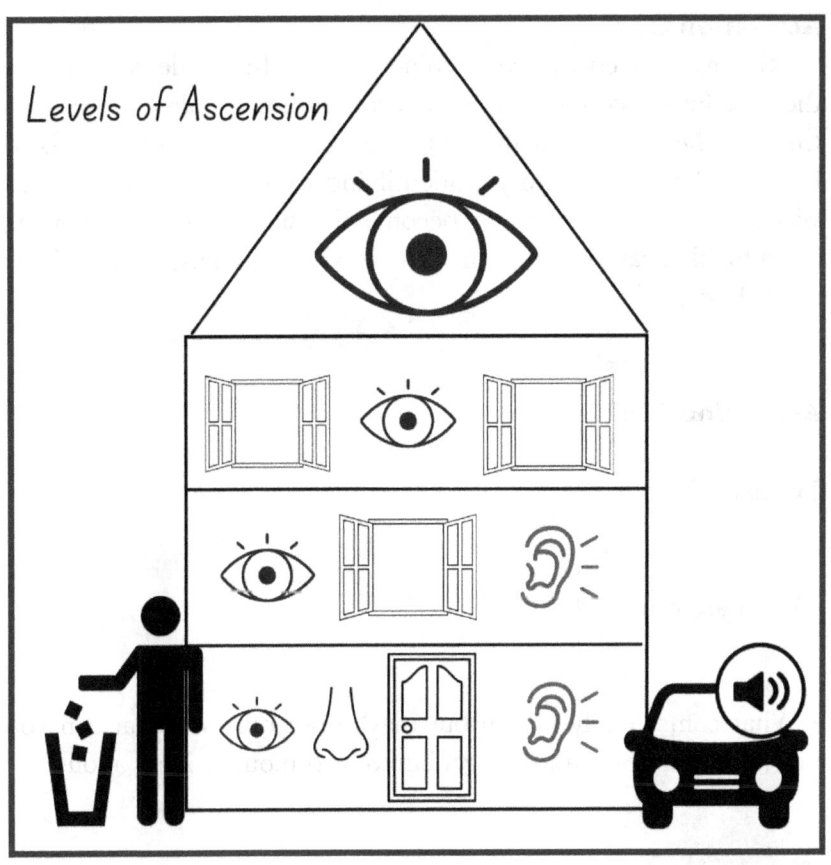

Activation One:

Sit cross-legged with your spine straight. Inhale deeply through the nose for 4 seconds, hold for 7 seconds, then exhale for 8 seconds through the nose. As a thought arrives, witness it and then focus back on the breath. Are you identifying with the thoughts as who you really are? Or can you become the silent observer, allowing them to fall away? Use this any time you feel you need to come back to the body.

Activation Two:

Journal below:

- What are you good at?

- What comes easily to you but maybe not others? What can you talk about for hours and not get bored or run out of ideas about?

- What would you love to help others with and be paid simply to exist as?

- If you knew you would be supported, what would you do?

- How does it make you feel in the body? Is it scary?

- What do you need to release and integrate to become the person you truly know you came here to become?

Light Mastery

Jessica Lousie (Beal)

Jessica Louise is a certified and licensed meditation practitioner, Sound Therapist, and business mentor to healers, mystics, and alternative wellness practitioners globally. She is the creator of the podcast Light Body Activation on Spotify and Youtube. As well as an international best selling author in the Amazon title, *Entangled No More: Women Who Broke Free of Toxic Abuse and are Building Empires*.

In 2022, after the launch of Entangled No More, Jessica monetized on social media. She began teaching other women in the industry how they too could monetize and generate leads on social media. In addition to free Facebook learning communities, Jessica hosts global digital business summits, teaching even more women how to tap into their own unique gifts, and use manifestation and mindfulness to create personal and financial prosperity.

Before this she had invested tens of thousands of dollars into personal development and learning digital marketing from home as a solo mom to 4 beautiful children.

> *The greatest insight I have had of my life is that I am not my thoughts. I am capable of more than I give myself credit for often, and to be kind is the greatest treasure of all. Despite all of your suffering.*

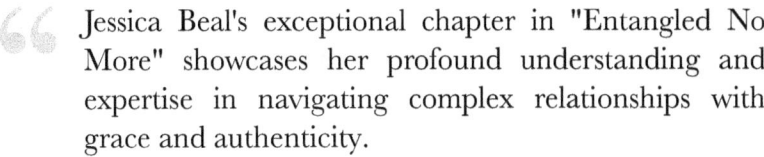

Jessica Beal's exceptional chapter in "Entangled No More" showcases her profound understanding and expertise in navigating complex relationships with grace and authenticity.

Katie Carey, Soulful Valley Publishing & Podcast

You can connect with her on Tik Tok Jessica Ignites, as well as on facebook at Jessica Louise.

Check out Jessica's current available offers at: https://pensight.com/x/jessicalouise

FIFTEEN

Echoes of Resilience: A Story of Recovery and Resistance

Xeres Villanueva

The Assault

When I finally looked at myself in the car mirror after my robber's fist hit the top of my nose and took my phone, blood was streaming down my face, oozing out. I screamed in horror and pain. My voice screeched to the top and then collapsed into crying. Disorientation filled my body, and panic rose from my being. With no phone to call anyone and unsure what to do, I found myself orienting by looking around as I caught my breath. As more adrenaline started to flood through my system, all I could think about was getting out of downtown LA. So, I left my spot and traced my steps back toward Echo Park.

It took me a moment to return to Echo Park as I tried to remember my turns and freeway exits. A rush of energy and adrenaline kept pumping into me as I traced back my steps to a farm in Echo Park called DragonflyHill Urban Farm, my workplace. I finally turned to Douglas St. and found parking near the Dragonfly-Hill location, which is a 100-year-old restored duplex with a front yard and a back yard. I sat alone for a moment with all the fear, shame and anger tumbling inside. After a moment to myself, I got out of the car, crossed the street, and walked to the door, pressing the doorbell on the door.

Please answer the door, I thought pleadingly

So many things were racing through my head. My face and hands were still covered in blood. The silence was so loud at the moment. My nerves were all over the place. Then, I heard footsteps getting louder and louder until the door opened. Drew, my friend, activist comrade, and my then employer, appeared at the door. When he saw me, he was shocked to see me back with blood on my face.

"What happened?" he asked as he ushered me into the house. He then took me upstairs to the restroom and their master bedroom, where he and his partner, Sue, slept.

"Someone opened my car door, punched my face on my nose, and took my phone," I replied, still afraid. "I need help calling my mom and dad."

At this time in the assault and robbery experience, I was filled with a combination of shock, a tremble and outrage stemming below the surface. The surreal nature of how this incident came to be was unreal at that point. Only moments before this took place, I had been in a volunteer staff meeting for a public art series program called Tuesday Night Cafe, spending time talking about how we wanted to start the upcoming season. I was a volunteer staff member at the time. After the meeting was finished, I returned to my car and chilled for a bit, looking up the Facebook event page for a friend's late-night Cupcake Wars' theme party to find the address.

Next thing I know, I am back at the duplex, sitting at the dining table, eating leftover food for dinner with my mom, her boyfriend at the time, and my friends, Drew & Sue, trying to explain what had just happened to me. My mom kept thanking Sue and Drew for helping me. During that moment, I felt moved that people important to me were coming together for me. At the same time, shame and embarrassment appeared. The rest of the night was both a blur and a rush. My family returned to Burbank, which is 15 to 20 minutes away from Echo Park by freeway, and drove around the city to find an urgent care center. There was no place that was open, so we had to return home until the next morning.

Seeking Justice & Recovery

"So, you did not go to the police station?" a LAPD officer asked on the other line.

"No, I didn't. I went to my friend's house, and I was bleeding from the top of my nose," I tried to explain.

"You should have done that first," he interrupted, abruptly.

The journey to addressing and recovering from the incident started with a mixed bag. The urgent care we found to help us the following morning was amazing. I was able to have the cut on the top of my nose re-stitched so that it would stop bleeding and start healing. On the other hand, connecting with the LAPD to get them involved or even to report proved to be infuriating. I was constantly interrupted and talked over every time I tried to tell my story, especially after I mentioned that I just went back to my friends for help. The officer on the other line was annoyed that I didn't go to the police station first to file a report. I was just irritated and belittled at this point. The more I tried to justify myself, the more I just got interrupted.

When I finally got to describe the attacker, I found myself quieting my voice when I mentioned that I couldn't describe him because I did not see his face. That's when the officer told me that it was just robbery rather than both assault and robbery, and they couldn't help me more. The audacity to say that while I am in urgent care! My mother asked me to give her phone back to her, giving the officer a piece of her mind.

When what happened to me was considered nothing more than a robbery, all because I couldn't identify my attacker, it hit me hard. The dismissal and gaslighting that happened as I was explaining myself and asking for help on filing a police report was like being punched in the face again: only with words and in broad daylight at the urgent care. There is a reason the Los Angeles Police Department is considered a mixed bag, at the very least, and a dysfunctional, oppressive institution at worst by several communities in Los Angeles County. From the 1992 LA riots to the department's questionable treatment of Black and Brown communities, not a lot of people look forward to encountering members of the police department.

So when I mentioned this to Sue when I returned to work after taking a week off, all she could say was, "So sorry. I knew something like that would've happened. They are not built to help us when we need them."

Despite the incident and knowing LAPD's checkered history, some family encouraged me to still file a police report anyway. Being in justice movement work and knowing history through both activist work and being a former law and government magnet student in high school, I was conflicted about filing the report. I did not want to feed the machine, and I didn't want to be turned down again. What got me to go and file the report anyway was a reminder that it is still worth standing up for myself and getting back what is owed to me regardless.

So I found myself in the police station in downtown LA with my independent living instructor, Ellie. Ellie and I drove together to the station so that I could get support and instruction to navigate the process of filing the report. The conversations during the drive were healing and full of truth.

What stood out is this: "You can honor that things did not get worse and still remember that you don't deserve what happened to you and that what you went through was awful and harmful."

My nerves were on hyper-alert during the whole time I filed the report, retelling my story and naming the facts to the officer who was there at the time. This was one of the few times where I braced myself throughout the whole experience. When it was finally over, I finally got my copy of the report. It still ended up listed as robbery rather than assault and robbery. I complained that this was still not right and that they insisted on leaving the assault charge out. I can recognize that I got the report to be used to apply for mental health support from the Victims Unit's services and still name that LAPD failed me. I can also recognize that I showed up for myself every step of the way.

During this process, I managed to get a week off until I got a new phone with my contact list updated. I utilized some of the meditative practice I learned from my martial arts training. A few weeks after receiving my police report copy and using it to file my application to the Victims Unit, I decided to still go to Chicago to attend the wedding of my former college roommate, knowing that I would have a lot of fun there. I wanted to still enjoy my life while processing what happened to me. I still wanted to be in touch with joy and connection.

Navigating the process of addressing the assault and robbery, both from the legal side and emotional side, and recovering from the situation lifted a veil that I didn't even know was there. It revealed that the current way of handling injustice and harm is woefully inadequate, especially with how the LAPD handled mine. I found myself facing the cultural wounds and stunted imagination that were coming up to the surface as I talked about my experience with public safety.

It took me a while to get back into my body. It started with joining a martial arts dojo and exercise boot camp. Then, my petition and application for mental health coverage through the Victims Unit went through and got coverage which led to being able to go to therapy and EMDR sessions with Dr. Elisabeth. It was conversations with Ellie and Sue, and my therapy work with Dr. Elisabeth, that helped me ground into my truth. It was necessary for me to recognize that even if nothing else happened to me, I am not required to minimize the impact the assault had on me. The process of filing with the police, recovering from the incident, and getting coverage for therapy paved a pathway for me to reclaim my own way of self-leadership and self-advocacy that is breaking the binary of either hyper-independence or neediness.

What is your journey in facing being unheard from others around you when going through something terrible that happened to you? It is not easy to keep advocating for yourself and searching for your support system when not a lot of communities and institutions can be loving witnesses, much less problem solvers. Speaking up may remain challenging to no fault of your own. Regardless of the outcome and process, you still deserve a life of dignity and integrity. You get to be witnessed and loved properly during your moments of being harmed and assaulted.

Activity

Weaving the relationship between the Heart chakra and a lower chakra of your choice can support you in holding your inner power.

Part of developing grounded self-advocacy your way is rebuilding your relationship within yourself and with your environment/surroundings at the pace of trust, capacity, and congruence. It will involve noticing the dynamic between context, perception, and sensations.

What you need:
- A safe place to write
- Paper and pen

1. Find a place where you can sit comfortably and write.

2. Check in and be present with what you are currently experiencing. Name and witness what you are currently experiencing: emotionally, mentally, and physically for at least 5 minutes.

3. Then lay out your palms and start imagining that the heart is one hand. Notice the color, shape and texture of the heart.

4. Then, do a body scan and notice which of the three lower chakras you are called to work with at the moment (solar plexus, sacral, or root). Once you decide which chakra to connect with, put the image and energy of that chakra on the palm of the other hand. Notice the color, shape, and texture of the chakra center.

5. From here, tune into your heart and ask: "What is needed right to be connected to my personal power?" Give yourself a moment and see what comes through. Whatever came through, even if it is nothing, is good enough.

6. Then, ask the chakra of your choice the same question. Give yourself a moment and see what comes through. Whatever came through, even if it is nothing, is good enough.

7. Next, imagine a figure-eight cord connecting the heart and the chakra of your choice.

8. As soon as the cord is formed, let the energies between them flow for a few minutes.

9. When you are ready, thank both of these energies for their messages and wisdom. Then, bring these chakras into yourself and let the energies settle into your being.

10. As you integrate these energies, notice the pace of your thoughts, emotions, and bodily sensations.

11. When you are ready, you may open your eyes and start writing down what you have experienced.

Xeres Villanueva

Xeres Villanueva has deep roots in community organizing, art and spiritual activism, mental health advocacy and social entrepreneurship. She has done culture change work with Inside Out Community Arts, Tuesday Night Project, WE Empowerment Center, Interfaith United for Justice and Peace and Social Enterprise Alliance. She facilitates discussion spaces, supports artists and creatives, and highlights community organizations and businesses. Her first start in culture change and healing work began in after-school tutoring and facilitating after-school art and enrichment programs in high school.

She has shared her insights and reflections on the intersection of spirituality, healing and justice on magazines and podcasts such as Chapel Probation, Inheritance Magazine, Divergent Magazine, Money Magic Podcast, Dragonfly Heart Medicine and Jesus Radicals. When Xeres is off the field of culture change and spiritual activism, she enjoys a cup of tea and cacao.

You can connect with her at https://linktr.ee/xvilla1228

SIXTEEN

Rebirth

Shannon Lord

Birth is not a sickness to be treated. It's not a thing to be fixed, improved upon, or restructured. Birth is a sacred journey that has been weakened and distorted through a millennia of shame, fear, oppression and ignorance. When people are told incessantly through powers that be, including medical professionals, media, parental authorities, friends, etc., that women's bodies (and all humans, for that matter) are inadequate and are in need of intervention, we can succumb to that belief even if our inner knowing tells a different story. This suppression of feminine power negates women's ability to align with her sovereign creator of life, not allowing her to navigate, steward and facilitate her unique "birthright". The power of choice, awareness and our magnificence are all within each and every one of us. The time is here to awaken to our purest power!

I am entirely aware that every birth experience is personal and unique, and can be interpreted in many ways and perspectives. I can only speak to my perspective and beliefs around my experience and what it has taught me along the way. Looking back on my birth experiences, I can see the unfolding of how a little piece of my soul was taken (or was given unknowingly by me) every time I gave my power away to another person or system.

These are my birth stories: the reclamation of my power as a sovereign woman, birthing mother and the Soul Alchemy that took place in the wake of it all.

Jackson

As I stepped off the elevator, onto the labor and delivery floor, I was engulfed by the distinct energetic smell of *hospital*, that of disease and pain that permeates every corner. I was 26, and Jackson was my first baby born. I remember the readiness to have him and the willingness to have a non-medicated birth.

Wanting to "have it all," the freedom to birth as I chose, and the "safety" of the hospital, I thought I had the best of both worlds. Already feeling like the outlier by not planning for an epidural right away, I sensed that my choice to have no medical intervention/non-medicated birth, unless it was an emergency, was not a notion embraced by institutionalized medicine.

Feeling scared, in pain and alone, I lay on a gurney in a darkened corner of what I can only describe as a sea of hospital curtains. Equating it to a holding tank in jail, I was scared and left alone to labor my first baby while I was being processed for admittance to the hospital. Once I was finally reunited with my husband in the hospital room, I was immediately stripped of my clothes to don the standard hospital uniform and put in bed, like all the other sick patients. All the while, I tried to get into a rhythm with the ebb and flow of my contractions. There were incessant disruptions that had nothing to do with my or my baby's immediate welfare. I was invasively jabbed with a needle in every vein in both my arms and hands while they were trying to place an IV. Meanwhile, feeling all the power I had to concentrate and flow through the contractions sapped away during an avoidable procedure that was again "for my baby and my safety." Now realizing the only purpose was for a possible medical emergency. The "just in case" inevitability of an emergency birth or c-section.

Feeling tied down to the bed every 40 minutes by the fetal monitoring device was intrusive. I would get into a rhythm with my rushes and make quick progress with the labor, only to have this precious space interrupted by having to change to a position that was not optimal for birthing. This constant intervention would break me out of my birthing spell. It was then and only then that my rushes were very hard to bear, and I had to use all my willpower to get back to a neutral place that would allow me to flow again with the waves of labor.

Seven hours from the time I arrived at the hospital, it was "time" to push: the phrase that is told to many birthing women. I question how someone else could be better at knowing this than the woman in labor. I've seen it time and time again in my own experience and with births I've witnessed in person. Hurry the birthing process along to include the mother, as well. I see it in the invasiveness of constant checking, monitoring, and forcing. Repeated internal checks for dilation (which can hinder labor more than help), induced births, elective c-sections, forceps, vacuum births, and episiotomies. Even in holistic approaches of acupuncture, herbs and the like.

I also can see it in counterintuitive parameters placed on every aspect of birthing. From how long gestation should be to how long each stage of labor should be and everything in between, the how, what, when, and where of the birthing process is scrutinized and structured in every way. I question how we can have such strict parameters on such a nuanced and entirely unique process. Every woman and baby have their own sacred dance of birth that cannot be replicated.

As my labor progressed to the pushing stage, a catheter was placed because my bladder was distended, which can be a barrier to "pushing effectively." Out of all the interventions, the placing of the catheter was one of the greatest blocks I believe to "effectively pushing" out my baby. Once my bladder was voided, I was not allowed the time I needed to gather my strength and was promptly told to start pushing right away.

The last and final intervention of the labor process was decided by the doctor. He would use vacuum extraction to suction the baby out. My ability to "effectively push" was directly linked to the sapping of my energy through the energetic tug of war throughout my labor. I was exhausted. It was my body's way of letting me know I needed to rest. Listening to my own intrinsic voice, those signals of when I needed to rest and when I could proceed were ignored by the people (hospital staff) that I thought were there to support me in the birth of my baby. So, at last, they won that tug of war. I had to succumb to another intrusion. I was told I could not push my baby out, and therefore I gave up trying.

Alas, my son Jackson was born. He was healthy; I was happy. Happy that my son was healthy, I should say. I was too beaten down, like so many women before me. Too sapped of my power to allow the heady mix of exhilaration of bringing a new life in the world and the pause of rejuvenation that comes as a natural evolution of empowered birth. I know this to be possible because this was my experience with Rylaigh, my second baby and birth experience.

Rylaigh (Pronounced "Riley")

It's not an exaggeration to say that there was a distinct difference between the birth of my first child and the birth of my second child. The difference was that now I was armed with the confidence of having a non-medicated birth with my first baby, Jackson, I felt that I was open to having a baby at a birth center. I hoped this could be a better fit, considering all that had transpired with Jackson's birth.

The lack of constant intervention and the ability to birth in water was very appealing. I felt that I could avoid the pitfalls of the hospital that were impeding the full experience of natural childbirth. Although, I didn't know if that would be the case. There were still questions. Was it me that was the reason for the struggle with my firstborn? Or was it really the environment? Later, I would find out it was both.

Rylaigh's birth center birth was indeed a lot less eventful. Upon arriving at the birth center, I immediately realized that the distinctive disease and pain smell of the hospital was profoundly missing.

Next, I was reassuringly aware that I would not be left alone at any time. My husband, Marc, was there every step of the way and even boldly caught Rylaigh as she was being birthed into the world. Being able to labor in the warm, comforting, weightless womb of the birthing tub was truly magical. It allowed me to be free to ebb and flow with my rushes and naturally make adjustments to positions, as well as any need for assistance, as a saw fit. I was invigorated after this birth experience with Rylaigh. Laughing and joking with Marc, I wondered why he was walking around with his hands up in the air like a surgeon does after they scrub in for surgery. He responded that he "had goop all over his hands, from delivering the baby." We were so overjoyed that we couldn't stop laughing.

Delaney & Cullem

They were both delivered at the hospital but with a midwife instead of a doctor. With Delaney, I was looking forward to another birth center birth, but halfway through my pregnancy, it was determined that my blood platelet count was not in the parameters to meet the standards for the birth center. This led to the devastating news. According to the medical model, I would have to go back to the hospital to deliver Delaney.

Coming from the harrowing experience at the hospital to the dreamy experience of the birth center, and then being told I would have to have another baby at the hospital put me in deep resistance. Looking back, I wish that I had dug deeper into that resistance. I know now that it was my warning sign, the red flashing light alerting me to take a different path, saying, "There is another way. You don't have to force yourself into something you know you are not in alignment with." I know hindsight is 20/20, and I don't disparage my former self for making the decision to go to the hospital and not have a home birth, which is what my soul was whispering to me.

Upon arriving at the hospital, it all came flooding in again. The solitude, the IVs, the interference, the pain, the frustration, the disempowerment. This state led me to be admitted to the labor and

Rebirth

delivery ward, only to be released two hours later because my labor had stalled.

I was given the opportunity to go home, and I jumped at the chance. It's where I truly wanted to be. I had silenced myself by not admitting my true feelings about going to the hospital, which stopped my labor completely. Had I known at the time that I had the power to do that, I could have harnessed that power to reclaim my birth process and refused to go back. I could have listened to myself when I had the wish, the dream to home birth, turning towards myself and honoring my true wishes. I didn't see that as an option at the time.

I went home and had a beautiful bath, which was all that I was craving at the time. I had to set my intrinsic knowing aside to force myself to acquiesce to the hospital, instead of giving myself permission to lean into my own empowerment. By turning away from myself, I fell into numbness and indifference about the whole birth process. Feeling very much the victim, I thought I had no other options.

I swallowed my integrity within myself and begrudgingly went back to the hospital, praying again for a quick delivery. My prayers would not be answered. The birth with Delaney was my longest and most painful birth. I didn't have as many interventions this time around. I guess I would attribute that to having a midwife making decisions for me instead of a doctor. I was grateful for that at the time.

At this point, my resources were depleted, and all the internal battling took a toll on my emotional energy stores. I succumbed to the pain that is so synonymous with childbirth. All that kept going through my head and several times verbalized to the midwife was that "The pain is too much to bear," "I'm not supposed to be here," "This isn't the way it's supposed to be," and "Something is wrong!" I felt like a trapped animal in a cage, knowing this was not my home, I was not safe, all the while lacking the will to fight against my captors. This phrase would ring in my head years later as an anthem to my hospital births.

By the time I had my fourth baby Cullem, I succumbed to this numb victim mentality and didn't fight the suggestion to stay at the hospital. I was grasping for whatever looked like the most holistic version of birth that I could have envisioned at the time. That looked like no epidural and a doula at the hospital. The spark of soul recognition was there in what I felt I had control over, but everything else was numb and robotic.

Looking back, I steeled myself for what could be the most magnificent and magical experience of my life. Don't get me wrong; the birth of my children will always be a profound moment in my life. I cherish the day they were born, bringing with them the bloom of new life and budding possibilities.

I can't say that my birth experiences did not shade my evolution through motherhood. The reoccurring themes of disempowerment would cycle back around time and time again, showing up in many facets of my life. My birth stories reflect this cycle that started way before my children were born. Reflecting on those moments, it's evident that I was not just screaming out in pain for myself but for all my birthing sisters who came before and will come after me. All of us shouting in unison, "Something is wrong!" "Something is wrong with the way society sees birth." "Something is wrong when women are being traumatized by birth." Something is wrong when the very essence of birthing isn't a place of empowerment, where women can be a revitalizing resource of their own innate power." "Something is wrong when the sacred act of bringing life into this world is stripped away by institutions negating the very process in which it was intended".

I know in today's society, my words are bold. They are not the norm and can be looked upon as radical and will cause waves. Going against the system can be jarring but completely necessary for women to tell their stories and speak out against oppression in any form. I ask you, if my words have stirred up any emotion, unearthed any feelings, what will you do now that the bell has been rung? What will you do with the fire that has been stoked inside of you?

It is my passion and privilege to traverse the inner landscape of our human experience, holding the mirror up against myself and allowing the space to support others in doing the same. I am building a new awareness of the capabilities and capacities within us all. I love working with the feminine power that resides in all beings. It is my hope that everyone will someday if not today, see the brilliance of their light and let it shine for the world to see!

When have you heard a message from your soul and ignored it?

What did you learn from this experience?

How can you listen to the calling of your soul in the future?

Shannon Lord

Hello! I'm Shannon Lord, a soul gypsy wandering the universe, exploring, playing, crying, laughing my way through this world in hopes to live life to the fullest. So far, within this lifetime, I've had the privilege to be a daughter, wife, mother, friend, student, follower, leader, activist, muse, and creator. I have a passion for this world and the beings that inhabit it. My dream is to open up within ourselves the way for all of us to experience the expansiveness of themselves through the connection to earth and their power within.

Insta - @embodied_path_sd
FB – Shannon Lord

SEVENTEEN

The Way Back

Susan Bennett Fisher

When I reflect on my life, I see a paradoxical journey—filled with fortune and goodness and laced with pain and despair. I see triumphs and success interrupted and rearranged by failure and trauma. How can so much good, and so much challenge, exist side-by-side, and where has it led me? When did I first know that I have a purpose? How did I lose track of that knowing, and how did I find my way back?

This is a love letter to my younger self, a celebration of the journey, and the re-discovery of my purpose.

Dear Susan,

There are layers of life that will obscure your purpose, squash your innate power and make you wrong for the gifts that you offer. I know as you experience life and the layers pile on, that it remains hard to connect with the sense of worth and value that are innately present. This letter will remind you of your earliest memories, moments where you knew your significance. It will show you how

The Way Back

the journey that you took layered pain, doubt, and manipulation on so heavily that you lost track of who you are. Most importantly, it will remind you of the pathway that your body's wisdom provides.

There were moments of magic when you knew something important and significant was happening—but no one around you seemed to share your experience. You often felt all alone, unable to understand why you feel and experience things that others don't.

Remember the night when you were 10, you got so angry with your sister that you punched her in the arm as hard as you could? Mom sent you to your room, of course. When you climbed out onto the gutter outside your window into the starry night, you felt your place in the universe. That was when you first knew that you had a greater purpose. The universe told you, that magical night, that you had a destiny, but to achieve it, you would have to learn how to use your incredible power for good.

Remember your experience at 16 in the Jewish Holocaust Museum in Tel Aviv? As you wandered the harrowed and hallowed halls, you were lost in the deep, sorrowful energy. The energy from the piles of shoes, the hair, the stories, swirled in and around you. Your family seemed almost unaffected, and comparatively, ran through the museum. For you, the energy of all those lives cut short imbued you with a sense of urgency and purpose to make your life matter.

Remember your teenage experiences in the Cathedrals of Europe—as you entered each one, you were filled with the sense of purpose and power contained in the stone walls, pietas, and stained-glass window masterpieces. You didn't understand why the family was not changed by the flow of information from these seemingly inanimate historical objects. For you, the energy instilled by the creators took over your being, informing and shaping you. You learned to know the wonder, awe, and majesty of source through these experiences. You felt both your significance and insignificance. The energy emanating in the interiors of these massive cathedrals permeated your body, catapulting you into the paradox of existence. As you stood there, and felt everything resonating in your chest, you accepted the knowing into your body: the knowing of a greater purpose to who you were meant to be.

All of these moments, so true and real for you, were there to anchor this sense of purpose into your being so that as you traveled your journey through life, repeatedly getting knocked off the path of your purpose, you would have something to hang onto. These moments and these memories would keep your knowing of your purpose alive.

Now, let's go back to the time, the darkest before dawn, when you hit the lowest low, a time when you felt the most lost. I know it's not fun to relive that part of your life, but it is important to understand how you felt during that time so you can acknowledge your power and ability to rise, Phoenix-like, from the ashes. Let's go back and start the journey from our 37th birthday:

Morning

You wake up on your 37th birthday with that familiar pit of nausea in your stomach, wondering what will overtake you today. You preview your day: rise, shower, prepare your two daughters for preschool, and drop them off at the start of your two-hour commute from home in Santa Cruz to Emeryville. You sigh and take a deep breath, feeling totally overwhelmed. With all these responsibilities, you are carrying the weight of the world on your shoulders.

Running two bed and breakfasts, both phoenixes themselves, resurrected from historic relics, trying to be a charming get-away for wealthy Silicon Valley weekend warriors, put a thousand pressure points on you. You are despairing about your children's youth as they are raised by one babysitter after another. Your husband is ostensibly "taking care" of things. But deep inside, your truth-telling soul is flipping over uncomfortably at your willingness to deny the dire nature of your circumstances.

You think to yourself–How did I get here? The refrain from a Talking Heads song plays in your head. You remember the prophetic night you first heard it while driving late fifteen years earlier. At that time, it had felt strangely portentous. In your mind, the words had morphed into your own version of the haunting melody.

A chill goes down your spine as you remember the feeling. "What is going on? I have done everything that was asked of me. How can this be my life? I went to Brown University, studied Mathematical Economics and Computer Science, worked on Wall St., got an MBA and MA in International Studies from the top business school in the country, and had one great job after the other. I married a smart, fun, athletic, handsome, and ostensibly loving man and had two beautiful daughters. Why did the formula not result in the promised outcome, a loving happy family, financial comfort, and professional success? At what point did my life go from potential to nightmare, and how did I not notice? How did I not realize the life planned for me by others was not my true path?"

A Not-So-Gentle Progression

Carpooling back home from Emeryville, chatting with your boss, you remark how much you feel like you did in the early stages of pregnancy, nausea, shakiness, lightheaded dizziness. You chalk it up to stress.

He says, "Well, maybe you ARE pregnant."

"No," you say, "I'm on the pill, and the vasectomy is planned. It's not possible."

Unable to shake the nagging possibility, you stop on the way home and pick up a pregnancy test. After peeing on the stick, it turns a bright shade of blue before you are done. Your heart sings. Filled with joy, this is the best birthday ever, and another beautiful soul is to come into your life. But the joy was overshadowed quickly by the mounting challenges.

Your husband does not want you to keep this child. He grows more and more sick with his addictions. He is a happy high and a mean sober. This makes it impossible to communicate. The relationship grows uglier.

Months Later

Four months pregnant, the phone rings. You hear your boss's voice as if in a nightmare.

"Yes, Susan, I am sorry. We have to lay you off." You feel, at some level, that you had brought this on yourself. The pit of fear grows to paralyzing cavernous depths.

Later the doctor calls. "You have gestational diabetes and have to go on a special diet or face insulin injections"

Your husband is nowhere to be found, emotionally, physically or spiritually. You separate from him in a vain attempt to dampen his caustic influence on your soul and your daughters.

Your life unravels even more.

The Summer - the Good, the Bad, and the First Steps for Change

Your daughter is born. Only the doctor and you are in the room when the shiniest light you have ever experienced pops out. She looks at you: She has no hair and bright blue eyes. How is it that she is already taking you in and looking for you to see her, and she is just born? Soon, you will find out why each daughter is so different.

No dark hair and dark eyebrows like her sisters. You know she is yours, but this is a new model. You feel a sense of joy and hope. You are grateful that she is here and starting her journey, and feel a deep need to make it safe and good. You feel sorrow that she has come into the world in the middle of a tempest and resolve to make it better.

You keep trying to make it all work. Your co-dependence allows you to give your husband more chances. You get a new job, good pay and local. It relieves some of the financial strain. But once again, you are not the one raising your daughters day-to-day. It causes you great pain.

You start going to Al-Anon and begin to realize that other people have tougher things going on than you do. But at some level, this makes you feel worse. This shouldn't be happening to YOU.

You're smart, educated, and attractive. You think "I did my good-girl routine. I should have it all. They promised."

You keep going to Al-Anon and learn more about your family history, and the impact of addiction, co-dependence and abuse. Oh! This is how you got here. Unbeknownst to you, you were raised within this model. It's not about you, it's about your daughters. It's time to break the chain.

Recovery

Looking for a new career you found The Coaches Training Institute and started their leadership and Life Coaching curriculum. At the first leadership retreat, you were desperately trying to look good, to keep anyone from really seeing you. All the while, inside you beg to fall all the way apart so that you can put yourself back together the way your soul wants you to be.

"You are in for a big treat today," says your leaders' assistant. He won't breathe a word about it, but you can feel the anticipation in his body.

You enter the meeting room; a couple is there. They begin to describe a discovery about humanity–there are nine physiologically different kinds of people and there is a physical process to identify which kind you are. You are intrigued. They invite one of your leadership tribe mates up, explaining what they are going to do. You see them push oddly on the person, and then tell them something about themselves that seems to make sense to them.

At your turn, the teacher stands in front of you. She does some gentle pushes. Then she asks you to bring your arms in close by your sides and lift your chest. You like the feeling as she pushes with more vigorous energy. You feel strong, confident, at ease. She tells you that you have Natural Number 6.

As you continue watching the experiences, something is fundamentally different in your body. Instead of simply observing people get identified, you feel something new. It feels like the rush of their souls as they come into alignment with their bodies. With each rush, you are overcome with tears. They are tears of remembering, of relief, of beauty and overwhelming joy-filled energy. It is as if the floodgates to your soul have been opened to consciously receive.

The other teacher comes over to you and tells you that if you expand your chest and meet the energy as it comes in, you will have an easier time handling and understanding the rush of energy. You take deep breaths, keeping your chest expanded. You notice that others are not having the same response, except for those others also identified as 6's. You are blown away.

Everything in your life that had not made any sense begins to click into place. You scan over the powerful experiences from earlier in your life, recognizing how distinctly personal they were to you. Despite the many activities shared by family members, no one seemed to be having the same experience as you. You were so worried that there was something wrong with you.

The explanation of how the physiology of your body works gave you a physical way of connecting to your spiritual nature and a posture in which you could be your most powerful self. You begin to understand that your reality is a gift and has a purpose, that is magical and important.

You also began to realize that your children's father spent your entire relationship attacking this part of you, removing your trust and confidence in who you are at your core. You realize that being different from your family is your special gift. You are supposed to be that way, and nothing is wrong with you.

In that moment, you knew that you would never be the same. This experience sparked a new journey for you that has led to self-love, acceptance, connection, authenticity, joy, harmony and the ability to create a conscious life.

Susan, this knowledge has been the key source of your personal transformation from a place of unconsciousness and pain (where you gave your power over to others) to a place of joy, happiness, and fulfillment. You have a partner in Martin (husband and Body of 9 Co-Founder) who you are more in love with today than ever, and who you trust implicitly.

Today, you know who you are.

You are learning how to develop your ability to activate the other Natural Numbers in your body into Superpowers so that you can become a more cosmic human. As your body-based skills develop you are more easily able to be with others. You can hear and receive the gifts and wisdom of others. You no longer feel alone. You understand how you fit in, and you value yourself and the contribution you make to your family, your community, and the world at large. You feel very grateful to have found that greater path that you knew was coming.

Honestly, Susan, I wish you hadn't needed to go through what you experienced, but every step was part of your learning, part of who you have become. There is no hurrying the transformation process. There is no secret recipe. It takes courage, commitment, willingness, desire to change and grow and awareness of yourself and who you are. Recommit every day to your purpose and recognize how lucky you are to be where you are today.

With Love,

Your Future Self, Susan Bennett Fisher

In Summary: Body of 9 has had many names, many contributors, and much transformation. Learning to activate all nine Natural Numbers in our bodies has proved to create a sense of relaxation, ease, and happiness, as well as a sense of purpose, knowing ourselves, and understanding our gifts and how to offer them. It has also taught us how to receive the gifts offered by others, to know how to create together in community. Every aspect of who we are and how we relate to each other, ourselves and the world around us is now consciously informed by this understanding. It is both a context for understanding our human experience and a modality for healing and growing into what we are meant to be at the level of our nature. We hope you will consider exploring this part of who you are.

I suggest you write a letter to your younger self, inspired by my structure or of your own design. If you want to bring this into alignment on a holistic level, learning your Natural Number will help. For now, take time to center, anchor into your body, then allow yourself to pour love into your younger self.

Collapse and Lift Exercise

We teach our "Collapse and Lift Exercise" as a way of allowing your body to activate the Natural Number area, and provide the associated calming and strengthening experience that comes with this activation. You can do this whether you know your Natural Number or not. It works because we all move and balance naturally from the activated part of our body:

Either sitting on the edge of a chair or standing, allow your whole upper body to relax, rolling forward, letting all the muscles in the upper body relax. Take a breath in this relaxed position. Then as you breathe in using your natural way, rather than any way that you have been taught to breathe, roll back up. Make yourself as tall as you possibly can as you stand up straight with arms at your sides.

You will naturally have used your movement area to lift your body, this creates the calming activation of your Natural Number, helping you return to a more aware and present state that is your natural way of being. If you are deep in negative thinking you can repeat this several times, each time you will calm more deeply and get more present.

For a video of this exercise go to: https://www.bodyof9.com/lift

Susan Bennett Fisher

Susan Bennett Fisher and her husband Martin R. Fisher are pioneers in the study and research of the 9 Natural Numbers. With over 30 years of combined research and experience with Body of 9, their work has led to many discoveries and a deeper understanding of the importance, power, and impact of knowing your Natural Number and learning to consciously use this aspect of your body. Since 2012, Susan and Martin have been working together to identify over 8,000 people from around the world and to build and share the understanding of how the Body of 9 shows up in so many aspects of human experience. Today they work with Coaches and Holistic Practitioners to bring in new information and new abilities to perceive so that coaches can create a new playing field for their clients. Body of 9 adds evolutionary skills, tools, and awareness that change coaches and their clients forever.

https://bodyof9.com/

EIGHTEEN

Finding My Inner Compass
Tracey Peffer

I thought I had my life all figured out. I had been happily married for 37 years, raised three daughters, and built a successful career as a mortgage broker.

But I still had the feeling I was supposed to be doing something more.

One day, I found myself drawn back to a memory from my childhood. When I was 8 years old, my world was shattered when my younger sister was hit by a car and killed. Even though Colleen was no longer there, I still felt a profound connection to her. She would visit me at night in my dreams. We'd hold hands and play in the waves on the beach. It was as if she never left.

Was this really just a dream? I didn't think so. It seemed so real.

Although I sensed the profound significance of these dreams, when I told my family about them, they dismissed me, telling me that I had a vivid imagination. Not only did they refuse to take my spiritual side seriously, they even put a Ghostbusters sticker on my bedroom door! Their message was clear. So I ignored my dreams and shut my spiritual side down.

But, years later, after my daughters moved out and that part of my life was over, I began to question everything I had once dismissed, everything I had been too afraid to embrace.

I started asking myself, "What is my purpose?" "Why am I here?"

These questions led to the beginning of a whole new life.

One day, I heard a voice telling me to go to a used bookstore to find a book I'd been searching for called "Awaken the Spirit Within." The old me would have ignored that voice. Instead, I went to the store. When I arrived, I found out that someone had just dropped off that book!

I stopped ignoring my dreams. Suddenly, I found myself waking up regularly at 4 o'clock in the morning to dreams of premonitions that came true. I dreamt that my car's right front tire and door fell off. The next day, I witnessed a car lose its right front tire and door. Then I had a dream about driving in the desert and passing a horrible accident where dozens of cars were burning. Two days later, I heard on the news that dozens of cars were burned in the desert when a wildfire spread on the freeway.

One night my grandparents, who had passed away decades earlier, woke me up with a tap on my shoulder, and simply said, "It's time." They appeared clear as day and were standing next to my bed holding hands. I wondered what they thought it was time for. Then I remembered that my oldest daughter Natalie was expecting, and her due date was coming up. Not wanting to wake her, I waited until 8 a.m. to call. My daughter told me that she had woken up at 4 a.m., the exact time my grandparents came to visit me, experiencing painful contractions. She delivered a baby girl later that day.

I began taking classes to tap into my third eye and develop my abilities as a psychic and medium. Switching from being a mortgage broker to being a medium was not easy. As a mortgage broker, I was used to dealing with concrete things like spreadsheets and square footage. As a medium, I had to learn to let go of any control and let things come to me. And I learned in this profession, you need to trust and surrender to the process. This was all so foreign to me. But the more I learned, the more fascinated I became.

One day, I signed up for a Psychic Intuition & Medium Workshop class. I was the first to arrive and found a seat in the front row. As I waited for others to join me, I opened my notebook and wrote down the date, the class name, and the course title. Then I found myself writing the word "Lilydale" in large letters.

Lilydale was a town in New York where a lot of mediums lived. I had just finished reading a book about Anne Gehman who was a famous medium who lived in Lilydale. If I ever got the chance, I wanted to visit Lilydale and meet Anne.

A petite lady sat down next to me. I thought it was strange that she had chosen to sit there even though the room was filled with empty seats. She told me that her name was Ellen. When class began, Ellen and I worked together on several exercises. One of them was called, 'Finding your inner compass.' We learned that your inner compass is your true essence, the all-knowing part of you, 'your soul'. By connecting with your inner compass and your soul you can align yourself with your highest potential and fully express yourself.

This was so incredibly cool. How was I just finding out about this?

When it was time to break for lunch, Ellen told me she had a plane to catch and would be leaving early. She handed me a business card and said, "You're welcome to come stay with me if you are ever in New York."

"Where in New York do you live?" I asked.

"Lilydale," Ellen replied.

I couldn't believe it! I had just written down the town's name in my journal because that's where I wanted to visit.

And now I had an invite.

This gave me goosebumps. It felt like a sign from above.

Two weeks after class ended, I reached out to Ellen, and we scheduled the visit.

When I arrived in Lilydale, it felt as magical as I'd hoped it would. I found Ellen's home. It was a lovely home on a quiet street. I felt something in the air as I approached the door to knock. I somehow knew that a big moment in my life was here. Ellen smiled

Finding My Inner Compass

when she opened the door, greeting me as if we were long-lost friends.

When she invited me in, I was immediately blown away. The entry was filled with pictures of celebrities, presidents, and spiritual leaders. I soon learned that Ellen was a retired White House correspondent. She was also an integral part of the town of Lilydale; she knew everybody. It felt like the universe had connected me to Ellen to show me that I could be both a businesswoman and a spiritual healer.

I asked Ellen if she knew Anne Gehman. "Oh yes," she replied, "We were very good friends. Anne just passed away, but her daughter is in town staying at her house. Would you like to meet her?"

The next day, we visited Anne's home. We met one of Anne's daughters, who graciously answered my questions about her mom. During that weekend, Ellen introduced me to her friends, many of whom were psychics and mediums. Visiting Lilydale and seeing a town filled with people who were spiritual like me gave me the confirmation I needed to continue my journey. I realized then that pursuing a career in the mystic world could become a reality.

I returned home ready to establish myself as a medium and psychic. My first step was to start putting myself out there. There was going to be a psychic fair in my neighborhood, so I signed up to give a 30-minute presentation. I had no idea what to talk about. Then I realized that I wanted to help people find their inner compass. If I could teach others what I learned and they could find their inner compasses, I'd be helping others lead a more meaningful life.

On the day of the presentation, my stomach was fluttering, and I felt sick. I was comfortable giving presentations about mortgages, but this was a whole different world. Could I do this?

My presentation was standing-room-only. I was overwhelmed by the reality that so many people had come to hear what I had to say. They believed in me! It felt as if in this moment the reality of the profound spiritual transformation I'd experienced was the reason I was standing in this room.

I couldn't speak. Worse yet, I began to cry. This was not how I had pictured this moment.

Then something within me said, "You've got this! This is your time to shine."

Then I began to tell the story of how I had dream premonitions that came true and how my life had shifted from being a mortgage broker to being a healer in the spiritual world.

I shared my experience of discovering my inner compass with the group and then taught them how to find theirs.

When I embarked on this journey, I asked myself, "What is my purpose?" and "Why am I here?" By the time the class had ended, I was confident in my ability as a healer and my capacity to bring people together to teach them powerful life tools.

I now understand that my purpose is to help others find their true calling and life's purpose.

You may think you have your life all figured out. But life has a way of surprising us. The universe sends us signs and subtle messages, leading us toward our true path. If you're open to listening, you may just experience the profound magic the universe has to offer.

Finding your inner compass exercise.
Your inner compass is your true essence, the all-knowing part of you, 'your soul'. By connecting with your inner compass and your soul, you can align yourself with your highest potential and fully express yourself.

Why would you want to connect to your inner compass?
Have you ever had a big question that you want answers to, and no matter how much you try to weigh your options in your mind, you just can't get the clarity you need? You even try asking your good friends but the advice you get from them is to "follow your heart". Tapping into your inner compass helps bring clarity during these times of confusion.

Finding My Inner Compass

How do you connect to your inner compass?
To access your inner compass, a few strategies I've learned are to clear your mind, take some deep breaths, send gratitude to your heart space, and then set the intention that you want to connect.

Ready to begin? Follow these 5 steps:

1. **Focus on your breath.** Take some long inhale breaths in through your nose and long exhale breaths out through your mouth. I recommend doing 3 or 4 deep breaths. Breathing deeply signals to your brain that you're shifting from an 'alpha' awake state to a 'beta' relaxed state, which is the state in which you can attune to your inner wisdom.

2. **Place your hand on your heart space.**
As you place your hands on your heart space, really feel into your heart. Send gratitude to yourself for things in your life you are thankful for. Then, set the intention that you are seeking clarity and need help finding your inner compass.

3. **Place your hand on your solar plexus.**
This is the area a couple of inches above your belly button. This is where you will connect with your inner compass.

4. **Start with a simple question to confirm how your compass works.**
Ask yourself a Yes/No question that you already know the answer to find what way your compass moves for Yes and No. Make sure it's a question with a definitive yes or no answer.

For example, I would ask, "Are my eyes blue? rather than "What color are my eyes?"

"Are my eyes blue?" "Yes." I immediately feel a slight tug to the right in my solar plexus. I know that a tug to the right is my confirmation for 'yes.' Instead of a tug, you may feel a twitch in your eye. Ask a few more questions to which you already know the answer will be yes just to confirm the direction of your compass.

"Do I have a dog?" "Yes." (tug to the right)

Now let's try some questions to which the answer is no.

"Is my car purple?" "No." (tug to the left)

"Is my dog's name Ranger?" "No" (tug to the left)

You may also have questions where you don't feel a strong tug in one direction. This can mean different things. Either indifference or that there is no clear path at the moment. In these cases, I suggest asking the question again in a few days. Or ask the question a different way to see if the answer changes.

5. Ask a question you have been seeking an answer to.
The questions can be about your career, relationships, finances, etc. Some examples are: "Will I get that promotion?" "Am I in the right relationship?" You can also have fun practicing with your friends.

Tracey Peffer

Tracey Peffer thought she had her life all figured out. She was happily married for 37 years, raised 3 daughters and built a successful career as a mortgage broker. A series of dream premonitions, followed by some undeniable signs and synchronicities from the universe, changed her life forever and led her to a profound and life-changing spiritual awakening. Life has a way of surprising us. And if you're open to listening, if you're willing to embrace these magical moments and listen to whispers of your inner compass, you may just experience the profound magic the universe has to offer. Tracey Peffer's mission is to help you live a more purpose-driven life by aligning you with your higher self. She does this with you by helping you connect to your 'inner compass' and awaken your soul.

www.tapinwithtracey.com

@tapinwithtracey – Instagram/ Facebook

NINETEEN

Embracing Shadows, Radiating Light

Raeleen Castle

 **The wound is where the light shines through.
–Rumi**

To prepare my sacred space to let in light and love to channel messages, I begin by lighting a bundle of sage and allowing the smoke to swirl around me and my space to clear any unwanted energy. I set the intention for only the purest and most positive energy to channel through me as I type the words for this chapter and use my pendulum to identify which items are the chosen ones to create the altar to support me this day and with this task; a photo of my Mother being the ancestor to guide me, a print of an owl to share wisdom, a variety of crystals in an array of shapes and sizes and colors each bringing its own power shimmering in the candlelight. One candle had a cylinder of glass around it coated with black smoke smudges. I always noticed them, but have chosen not to clean them off. This time, however, I heard the message to remove them. For a moment, I considered not doing it because it takes time and effort, but I heard it again and knew that this was not only something I needed to do but a metaphor for something greater.

Inspired to clean the glass, I realized this was such a simple example of what happens every day. We have smoke smudges in our life we become used to being there, like a build-up of our shadows. Sometimes, it's not until we clear the darkness that we can fully let the light in—or in this case, out. For a long time, I struggled to let my light in or out because of the programming that I was letting hold me back. Limiting beliefs I wasn't even aware of were running my life. Feelings of fear and unworthiness kept me from what I wanted. I was always in my head, thinking, planning, and controlling. Not always in a constructive way, but more often than not judging and comparing, not just others, but more importantly myself.

In high school, I loved English classes, I felt like I was good at them. I dreamed of being a writer, an author writing novels in New York City. I lived in a small town in Canada, and the local newspaper was hiring a writer. I put together a resume and samples of my writing as well as references from my teachers and submitted them. That took a lot of courage. I was excited and nervous. I got a call and was offered to write a piece! I was amazed, it was an opportunity to start on my journey of becoming a writer! Except the fear and doubt grabbed hold tight. The voices were telling me that I couldn't do it and all of the reasons why—that everyone would be watching me and waiting to criticize me and watch me fail. It felt safer not to try at all, so I turned down the opportunity and put the dream of being a writer off for the time being. I thought about the dream now and then over the years, but did not take another chance to realize it until now; after many years of releasing limiting beliefs and wiping the shadows away so I could let my light out and share it with those who need it most at this time of awakening.

At the beginning of my healing journey, when I just couldn't feel how I was feeling any longer, I took my first step and started seeing a counselor. One of the first practices she suggested for me to try was mirror work. I was asked to look in the mirror and say "I love you" to my reflection. I just couldn't do it. I would just cry instead. This was the first time I realized that I didn't love myself. Not loving myself trapped me in a pattern of trying to control everything, being angry and frustrated, criticizing myself for not being a good parent, and all the other negative things I told myself.

I first had to see these feelings and beliefs, then sit with them.

I asked: Do I want to continue to feel like this? How would I rather feel? What would I rather do? What would I rather have? How would I rather experience my life?

There are so many ways to show up in the world, and I often get stuck in analysis paralysis: not sure which decision to make, and instead, not making a decision at all. Not moving forward and so staying in the same place. Sometimes, I didn't get the choice to make a change because the universe would force my hand.

My children and I were living in a dingy basement suite. I had left a relationship and our home, and had taken what I told myself was the best choice, but really I had made the choice based on the price of the rent, a scarcity mindset, and had compromised on so many other things. I knew that we needed to go, I was reminded of it every time I heard the rats in the walls, and when I drove a longer way to and from work than I really wanted. But I wasn't making any steps to remove us from the situation. For the first time in our area, we had a weather occurrence called atmospheric rivers. There were entire areas that were under water. Water flooded the basement suite we were living in. I had to make the decision that it wasn't safe and for us to leave. We moved upstairs temporarily, but the roof was leaking too! We needed 3 bedrooms, someone that would allow a dog and in our price range, ASAP. Our prayers were answered. We got most everything on our wish list, including a landlord that lived in the house and really cared about the building and us. We got what we deserved because the universe wasn't going to let us settle for less.

Into the Light

Today, I'm able to cry happy tears because I love myself and the life I have created.

I spent a long time releasing people and things that no longer served me so I could align with myself and find my people and communities. Now, I feel free to share who I am authentically, speak my truth and feel good doing it knowing that I am always safe and supported and everything is always working out for me.

On this journey, I have released fear, shame, guilt, unworthiness, and not-enoughness. Today, I can shine my love and light boldly and proudly, knowing my supportive community celebrates me. I love that I get to celebrate and honor them, showing their unique colors and spice. We are all one, and we are all here to have this experience together. I am grateful.

Thank you! Thank you for being you and being open to listening to your intuition that guided you to this book and read this chapter and receive the vibration of loving energy that I am sharing as you read these words.

What I've Learned

Shadow work is an ongoing journey. It's not one-and-done.

What we are experiencing and learning is for us to share with others to help them along their journey.

There are big T traumas and little t traumas. We often hear more about big T traumas like being physically or sexually assaulted. Obviously that is traumatic, and people are recommended to get help. Little t trauma: not feeling good enough, feeling judged, shamed or unworthy often isn't recognized, and we don't realize the detrimental effects it's having on us and don't think to get help. Learning to love yourself allows you to learn to love others, realizing we are all one and can have love for all.

The experiences that didn't feel so good at the time, the uncomfortable shadows, are actually happening FOR our own good and are necessary for our healing: The dark in contrast with the light. You can love yourself and give yourself grace, forgive yourself, and see things as an opportunity to learn and grow. Know that you won't always be in shadow; it's only for a period of time, and it's likely for a reason. Where can you find gratitude to create light in the midst of it?

I live my life now incorporating things that make me happy; understanding that it is how I feel that's most important to my frequency. I have created an entire morning routine, understanding it sets the mood for my day, and I end my day doing things that make me feel happy, too. Part of my morning routine is to pull a tarot or oracle card as guidance for my day. Today, I was guided to pull 3 cards. The first was the Emperor with the message that I lead in my world with confidence, harmony and generosity; and for me to step into success and rise, the world is mine! I read this card with happy tears and know that writing this chapter is something I am meant to do and is making a difference in people's lives. The second card was Paradigm Shift; release old beliefs and be open to new; go through uncertainty, release fear and conditioning, and embrace love by surrendering and trusting that what's happening is FOR me to bring me closer to peace, love, empowerment and happiness. The other message offers a healing affirmation likely meant for me and you: "I return to the truth that source flows through me. I am aligned." We move toward healing only when we acknowledge what needs to be looked at: our shadows, where we're disconnected from the source of who we are.

Part of my soul's mission is to write, yet I've held back, until now.

Sometimes we need to wait for divine timing or right fit. When I was invited to write in *Soul Alchemy*, I wasn't ready. I still had personal work to do as I felt I wasn't good enough and the other authors had more "worthy" knowledge and experience to share.

I told myself, "What could I possibly offer?"

These limiting beliefs came from my own unprocessed shadows. Since then I have done work around the shadows that have held me back. In my healing journey, I've come to realize I am meant to share what I've learned with others. My love, light, and learning can lead others to heal and be their best selves. When we release the stories that keep us small, we can share the truth of our own brilliance. We all have a unique story to share; no one is better or worse than another. We will all resonate with different people, but we are all meant to do this together and support one another energetically and with our voices because we all deserve this success.

What I would like to give you today is a mantra to say daily, once or more. I also recommend recording yourself saying it and listening to it in your own voice, and the best would be creating a loop and listening to it while you meditate or while you sleep. This is a great way to change the unconscious programming that is running in the background of your mind. Changing this programming will change your life!

Seeds of Change for Your Soul Mantra:

I am grateful to my ego for protecting me, but I am ready to release the fear and allow myself to trust and have faith and know true love: Love of myself, Source, and humanity. In this love, I am able to know that I inherently deserve everything I want. I plant the seeds of intention, I feed myself nourishment and love, I remove the weeds of limitation, and I rest and surrender, sitting back and watching the garden of my life flourish with effortless ease and flow. Thank you. Thank you. Thank you. So be it and so it is. I am open to receiving this or something better.

If the Seeds of Change resonate for you on your journey, I look forward to connecting with you as I bring this work and others forward in the future.

Raeleen Castle

Raeleen is a new author; finding her voice and spreading her vibration of love and light through the avenue of writing. She has been on a journey of learning to love herself, releasing her limiting beliefs and replacing them with empowering beliefs for some time now, and is helping those more recently awakening to do the same.

Raeleen has read many books, taken classes, and workshops, listened to podcasts for years and has much knowledge to share. She loves sharing the things she has learned in her experience, knowing intuitively what tool may be best for each person or situation. Raeleen is known best for her honest and direct, but always positive approach, which people appreciate. She models what she suggests; showing vulnerability. Raeleen is often called inspiring and told that people want to be more like her.

If you would like to learn more about Raeleen and how you can connect with her follow her at: https://linktr.ee/raeleencastle

TWENTY

Shakti Has No Shadow: Embracing Your Entire Being

Aurelia Corvinus

What if I told you that you don't actually have a shadow? Or if I had the audacity to tell you that, "Shadows are the monsters under the bed of your spiritual awakening."

Would you believe me?

Indulge me for a second; go and get a quarter or pound coin. Pick it up, hold it in your hand, and really look at it for a moment. You'll see two sides—one is the back, and the other is the head of a leader, forefather, ruler, or Sovereign. The coin is whole. You can flip it, but both sides are equal parts of a whole. The side that shows the Sovereign, for example, is not worth less simply because she has a different side. The "shadow" side or back is just part of the coin.

That, in a nutshell, is non-duality.

I spent 15 years of my life trying to make peace with my duality. How could I be so grounded and high-vibe one minute and absolutely crushed or even vehemently angry the next? I felt like I couldn't "stay in the light." I couldn't hold onto alignment. I was constantly disappointed in myself for "struggling" when in all actuality, I needed to lean into rewriting negative limiting beliefs, heal my trauma and allow myself to experience and even relish the full spectrum of human emotions. I was still a beautiful, complete soul

Shakti Has No Shadow: Embracing Your Entire Being

when I was angry. I was still a beautiful, complete soul when I was so mentally or physically exhausted I could not function productively. I was still a beautiful, complete soul when I cried from deep sadness. I was, and always will be, a beautiful and complete soul.

I spent my entire adulthood until the age of 39 desperately trying to figure that out.

Meditation was the key piece that helped me and found me like a Divine gift exactly when I needed it. You see, I didn't know how to find spirituality or even if I was spiritual. In 2020, I started meditating as a way to cope and process the pandemic. Meditation led to a path of self-compassion and self-acceptance. It was as if meditation was initially a triage for the gaping wounds I was carrying.

Through meditation, I found Vedic (traditional Indian) philosophy. There are many Indian schools of thought within Hinduism, Sikhism and Buddhism. One school of thought that resonated very deeply with me is called Vedanta.

Vedanta is a profound philosophy rooted in ancient Hindu wisdom, that introduces a captivating perspective on the nature of reality. At its essence, Vedanta is built on the idea of non-duality. Think of Vedanta as an exploration of Oneness, where the ultimate reality is seen as a singular, formless essence (Brahman) that transcends distinctions between individual souls (Atman) and the divine. Not only are you whole and complete as you are, but you are also Divine. You are the Universe, and the Universe is you. This is the basis for the popular "As above, So Below" concept.

Vedantic philosophy suggests that what we perceive as multiplicity or separation in the world is an illusion (Maya). To put it simply, Vedanta encourages us to look beyond surface-level differences and recognize the deep, underlying unity of everything. In embracing this perspective, the most popular school of Vedantic philosophy, Advaita Vedanta, guides seekers toward a profound realization of self-knowledge and an awareness of the interconnected, non-dual nature of existence. Essentially it means that every single part of you, every wound, every emotion, EVERYTHING is sacred.

When I sat with the concept of everything being sacred, it felt strange at first. The more I leaned into non-duality, the more I felt a deep truth. We didn't incarnate here on Earth to be perfect. We incarnated to experience the entirety of being human in a full spectrum experience, and fully open up to the beauty of that experience. Think of it like this: if you take a flower and hold a light in front of it, it casts a shadow on the wall. The shadow, though, is an illusion; it's not part of the flower. The flower is whole, whether it's in a light or whether it's in a dark room. The flower is the same. Only our perception of the flower changes.

That concept, if truly internalized, might make exhaustive shadow work completely unnecessary. Should one participate in introspection, meditation, healing, and more? Absolutely. Should one heal traumas that occurred in their lives? Absolutely. Are those traumas and perceived character "flaws" based on societal conditioning actually "shadows" that we need to retrigger ourselves to excavate from our psyche and soul, releasing all darkness? Absolutely not.

Perception skews your human experience, your Divine soul is limited in a physical incarnation, and your perception and perspective reflect that.

A great example of this is the energy of confidence. Let's say you see a beautiful woman in a restaurant. She's dressed very well, in a gorgeous dress, smiling, loud and bubbly. When she leaves, she walks out with her head high with a rhythm in her steps. Now, some may think, "Oh well, who does she think she is?" or "She's so vain!" Vanity is the perceived shadow aspect of confidence, but in reality, she could have grown up incredibly poor and worked very hard to cultivate wealth. She may have been terribly shy in school and spent years creating a self-image that brings her joy. Other people's perceptions and opinions are not the truth, and other people's perceptions and opinions are certainly not *your truth*.

For another example, let's look at Hinduism, one of the world's oldest religions. Its origins can be traced back several thousand years.

In the Hindu pantheon, Goddesses Durga and Kali emerge as living, energetic expressions of the ultimate feminine creative power of Shakti, albeit embodying distinctly different facets. Durga is the

Shakti Has No Shadow: Embracing Your Entire Being

protective Mother-nurturer, wielding weapons and riding a lion, symbolizing strength and compassion. Her sacred rage, vividly portrayed in creating Kali, transforms her embodied destructive energy into a force for rebirth and liberation.

Kali, with her dark complexion and formidable presence, represents the fierce transformative force of Shakti. Associated with time and destruction, Kali illustrates the necessity of upheaval for renewal. Durga birthed Kali from her third eye in an act of such deep sacred rage she saved the entire world through her creation of Kali. Their narratives, beautifully interwoven, reveal a dance where shadows are illusions, and that destruction can become a catalyst for creative rebirth. Kali is no less Divine or powerful than Durga, and both are worshiped and revered equally. There are temples for both Goddesses today in India. Durga does not need to "integrate" her shadow aspect of Kali. Kali is not a shadow aspect; both energies are equal, powerful parts of Shakti—a whole being. They are simply different aspects of the same being.

I believe that is how our human essence also works. We all hold many aspects. We are like a faceted stone. Light rarely touches all the facets at the same time, yet the stone still sparkles. All of those facets belong to the stone. The sparkly stone is one whole being.

Everything we encounter, we unconsciously view with our own programmed belief bias. What happened to you, what you believe, what you were told, where you grew up, and your childhood experience shape how you view everything; they contribute to a limited perspective of a much larger soul experience. Honestly, I believe that is all the modern new-age "Shadow Work" movement really is: a misguided human perception of that limited perspective causes us to label unhealed trauma, a trigger, or even a flat-out untruth as a big scary shadow.

When that clicked for me, I finally understood that the real shadow alchemy is realizing shadows don't actually exist. You are light. You are shadow. So go be both. Love both.

You are a whole Divine being, just as you are.

Sacred Acceptance Ritual: Embracing Non-Duality

Step 1: Preparation
Gather items for your sacred space: a white or gold candle, incense or sage for cleansing, a journal, and a blue pen. Find a quiet, comfortable space where you can be undisturbed for the duration of the ritual.

Step 2: Cleansing Ritual
Light the candle and the incense or sage. Take a moment to center yourself, focusing on your breath. As the smoke wafts around you, visualize any negative energy or limiting beliefs being released and transformed into positive, loving energy.

Step 3: Meditation
Slowly begin your meditation. Stretch and release any tension in your body. Sit comfortably and start focusing on your breath and allowing your mind to quieten. As thoughts arise, simply acknowledge them and gently return your focus to your breath. Allow yourself to sink into a state of deep relaxation and openness.

Step 4: Reflection and Journaling
After your meditation, open your journal and reflect on the following prompt: "What if I allowed myself to fully embrace the concept of my shadow simply being an illusion? How would my life change if I saw myself as a whole, divine being, capable of experiencing the full spectrum of human emotions without judgment or fear?"

Step 5: Closing
Take a few deep breaths, feeling the energy of acceptance and wholeness permeate your being. Thank yourself for taking this time to honor and embrace your whole and complete essence. Extinguish the candle and incense and say a gratitude prayer symbolizing the end of the ritual.

Aurelia Corvinus

Aurelia is an intuitive Artist, Mama, and Healer who channels her spiritual practices into her art and offerings. With a deep reverence for the Divine Feminine (Shakti) and a passion for exploring the depths of the human experience, her work is a mesmerizing reflection of the inner workings of the soul.

She can show you how to bring light into your life, heal your heart, make peace with your soul, and expand your perspective.

Drawing on the ancient traditions of Vedic philosophy, yoga, ceremony, ritual, and sacred self-care; Aurelia infuses her offerings with the transformative power of these practices. Her methodology is rooted in self-acceptance, and mystery of the natural world, as well as to the potency of our physical body and its capacity for spiritual evolution.

Currently invoking an alignment to her highest timeline. Aurelia is concentrating on her visual art, learning music and songwriting, discovering her edges, finding her muse, exploring sound healing, and diving deeper into sacred Mantra. She is stepping into the calling of spiritual leadership through group facilitation, courses, workshops, energetic activations, meditation, and one-on-one spiritual guidance. Aurelia is adept at multidimensional healing, crafting rituals, sacred living, herbalism, Ayurvedic Medicine, aromatherapy, personal creative expression practices, and making artisan wellness products.

Find out more at https://www.aureliacorvinus.com/

TWENTY-ONE

Dark Fire Rising: My Journey to Sovereignty

Lindsey Rainwater

An intense feeling bubbled up inside me. It was like something was trying to claw its way out of me, making me feel like there was some kind of horrific, spiny monster sitting just under my skin.

Except that the monster was me. A dark, rage-filled and venomous version of myself, barely restrained by my mask of flesh, was waiting for its opportunity to burst forth, howling and crying, and I would die.

I was, once again, lost in the landscape of a world that seemed to despise me. I was continually shown that I was "wrong."

My whole childhood, whatever I did, I was wrong. There was something twisted about me, no matter how hard I tried to straighten it out. I was constantly bombarded by authorities telling me who I needed to be, only to have that rug yanked out from under me. I was misled to believe these situations were somehow my doing.

It reached a point where I could not continue like this.

Now, I can't give you a date, time, or location. They bleed together: at home, at church, at a friend's house, at church, at sports practice, at church...

A blurry amalgamation of shame, pain, and oppressive

programming tried to press me down until I could not stand under its weight. The vicious system of control told me to stop being so weird and give in. Just follow the rules, and everything would be ok.

But… I don't know how to stop being so weird, and I'm not very good at following the rules: especially pointless, arbitrary rules that are only there to keep people small, scared, and groveling at the feet of those who benefit from control.

So when I found myself in that place, again, of feeling like I had the choice of scream or die, I prayed to whoever was listening.

I cried and said something like, "I don't want this. I don't want to be this person anymore. I want it to stop. I'm so tired. I am exhausted from this game. Please help me."

What I wanted–or at least what I thought I wanted–was to go to bed and never wake up again as this weird little person.

I begged my angels to take away this discomfort. The celestial beings I spoke to in my dreams understood me, didn't they?

Especially the gray one–he would help me through this painful mess. Right?

But this journey was not an immediate escape but a slow, determined march toward self-understanding and sovereignty. This sovereignty would not be granted by societal acceptance but claimed in the shadowed realms of self-discovery and spiritual communion with deities that worked in darkness.

I did not wake up as a reformed, normal, acceptable version of myself. While that was momentarily disappointing, I eventually began to realize what a gift I had been given.

It wasn't easy always being on the fringes. Leaning into my solitude did not suddenly make the disapproval of others painless.

And yet, as time went on, I asked why it mattered so much.

Why did it matter what I dressed like?

What was the purpose of telling children how they needed to act and think at all times?

Why did there appear to be some sort of overarching demand for conformity, to the point where if you did not fit the mold, others would attack you as though **their own** existence depended on it?

These were questions that began to haunt me, and I had more than my fair share of existential crises.

Then came the crumbling of faith. Not faith in something bigger–I had my angels and this Egyptian god that seemed to follow me around—but my faith in The Church began to implode under the weight of unanswered questions.

Why did we go to hell?

What kind of loving God would give me gifts and abilities, then eternally punish me for them?

How was it OK for adults to stand in front of a room of kids and tell them they would burn for eternity if they didn't follow the rules? That people they cared about would be ripped from them and tortured if those people didn't accept Christ as their one-and-only Lord and Savior?

Did those adults sleep soundly while I had panic attacks in the middle of the night?

When I talked to what few friends I had about these topics, they would brush them off or even shut the whole conversation down, as though I was risking the summoning of some nameless boogeyman.

As I got older–into the angsty, tumultuous phases of teenhood–I started leaning into the darkness that seemed like it was growing into its own entity inside my chest.

What was this beautiful darkness that so many people hated?

Why was there such fear and condemnation of the mythos and magic that had birthed so much of our history?

How come topics like death, dying, and getting eye-to-eye with mortality were so taboo, especially when combined with being able to perceive things that the people around me couldn't?

If God sent angels to those he had chosen for great things, why was I damned for speaking with them?

So, my awakening began—not with a scream, but with the quiet determination to question and challenge the totalitarian forces that seemed to press in from all angles.

Ultimately, my goal was to embrace the full spectrum of my being, darkness and all.

This was my path to sovereignty, a path lit not by the harsh light of conformity but by the soft glow of self-awareness and the Dark Fire of transformation. The Dark Fire is the force I discovered deep inside me, and its gentle yet destructive blaze has etched my path.

My journey away from conformity began with hesitant steps, a silent mutiny against playing by someone else's rules. I withdrew from the futile quest for approval from those who couldn't grasp what I was experiencing.

Delving into my passions—mythology, the paranormal, the mysteries beyond life—I started to see my uniqueness not as a flaw, but as a distinction.

My interest in the darker aspects of life wasn't an active rebellion so much as giving myself permission to embrace the themes of death, transformation, and renewal that have fascinated humanity forever and come with a heavily polarizing energy.

I came to realize that society's denial of death obscures the liberation that comes with **accepting** our mortality. This avoidance causes us to lose sight of what's important. Embracing mortality prompts us to reevaluate our lives, choices, and what we prioritize.

Why seek approval from those who benefit from us not being our authentic selves?

Why engage in pursuits that don't fulfill us?

Awakening to the power of death and transformation taught me that life's essence isn't found in fearing the end but in recognizing death as a transition and a teacher.

In embracing death and transformation, I embraced self-sovereignty. This wasn't about becoming **new**, but about peeling back societal expectations to reveal my authentic self. It took years of going back and forth with myself, wondering if these entities were real, or figments of a desperate and lonely imagination.

But eventually, I realized there were too many synchronicities for my experiences to be made up, and too many messages to ignore. So I allowed myself to assume that it was all real, and everything that had been revealed by these guides and experiences was meant for me.

Azrael (who the aforementioned gray angel turned out to be) and Anubis illuminated that recognizing death marks not an end, but a fresh start, teaching me that closures lead to growth and every ending to rebirth. On top of that, "deaths" and "rebirths" happen to us **all the time**.

This understanding shifted my view of my personal struggles. From the ashes of what I had seen as heavy burdens came the wings of my evolution.

This journey with the Death Deities was far from a plunge into despair. It was a quest revealing that embracing my shadow was crucial for sovereignty. They instilled in me the value of discernment, teaching me to identify what benefits me.

This process, rooted in love, involved thoughtful consideration of my choices and paths and emphasized growth, understanding, and authenticity. It kicked off the exploration of rabbit holes regarding faith and religion. I doubled down on my questions regarding the god of the Bible and the things I had been taught to accept: things that were often conflicting and felt **wrong** deep in my spirit.

I began by dismantling the doctrines I'd been trained on and trying to find the "man behind the curtain" that seemed to be running mainstream religion. All the talk about our loving God, and the feelings of acceptance and support I got when I prayed or felt "spirit" move in me, did not line up with this power-hungry, jealous, demanding figure that ruled The Church.

I realized that this being was not The Elohim. This was some other deity that had somehow gotten enough PR to become "God."

Then, I finally allowed myself to believe that when I die, my soul will not be delivered into the hands of an entity that makes up harsh, arbitrary rules and doles out eternal punishment in the name of "love."

I developed the courage to point out to people that if a human treated anyone I knew like the god of the Bible treated his followers, I would tell them to run far away and get a restraining order.

Further pushing the boundaries of the acceptable, I proclaimed that the angels are not tied to this entity–they are sovereign in their own right–and that I now have "friends on the other side."

I like to think that when Death comes, it will not be some

horrible experience of judgment and shame, but a warm welcome into the next leg of a weird adventure.

All of this took away some of the sting of death. The fear abated a little, and I was able to face it, hold its face in my hands, and give it a kiss. I unlocked my ability to be sovereign because I am, indeed, currently mortal.

As I navigated my path with the wisdom of Death Deities as my guide, I began to see the myriad ways in which society attempts to dictate our choices–to mold us into compliant shadows of ourselves. With each step taken in defiance of these pressures, with each decision made in alignment with my true self rather than the expectations laid upon me, I felt my sovereignty strengthened.

Embracing my sovereignty meant recognizing that the power to define my existence rests solely in my hands. It involved a profound acceptance of my responsibilities–to myself, to my Death Deities, and to the world.

Living as a sovereign being has manifested in countless ways, both big and small.

It has meant choosing careers that resonate with my passions, even when they diverge from the conventional paths to success.

It has meant ending relationships that stifled my growth and nurturing those that encourage mutual respect and understanding.

It has meant speaking my truth–or refusing to engage when I'm being baited–and standing firm in my convictions, even when faced with opposition or misunderstanding.

Yet, perhaps the most profound aspect of realizing my sovereignty has been understanding that it is an ongoing journey, not a single destination.

There are challenges and obstacles aplenty, but through the healing process, we discover how powerful we are!

Now, standing firmly in my own sovereignty, I extend an invitation to you, not just to observe from the sidelines, but to engage actively in your own profound transformation.

It's time to stoke the Dark Fire within. To nurture your own guiding flame so you can revel in every aspect of yourself–from the brightest lights, to the deepest shadows.

You do not have to discard the parts of yourself that society deems unacceptable or frightening. Rather, you can integrate these parts, recognizing them as essential components of your whole being.

Death Deities, those guides and guardians of the threshold, offer us a unique perspective on transformation. They remind us that embracing the unseen, as well as our shadows, is not an act of defiance but a declaration of authenticity.

Invoking the Dark Fire within is not a journey for the faint of heart.

It requires courage, resilience, and a willingness to explore the uncharted territories of your soul.

But know this: you are not alone.

There are others, like me, who walk this path alongside you, who have found in the darkness a profound source of strength, wisdom, and power.

Let us journey together, not away from the darkness but deeper into it, where we will find not fear but freedom, where we will discover not isolation but community.

Here, we will ignite not just the Dark Fire within ourselves, but within each other, lighting the way toward a world where every individual is the sovereign of their own life, free to live, love, and grow in the fullness of their authentic being.

In the end, this is not just about overcoming trauma or breaking free from societal constraints. It's about recognizing that within us lies a power vast and profound, that society has long sought to suppress.

In embracing our shadows, in questioning the structures that seek to define us, and in forging connections with the divine forces that guide us, we find **peace**.

Continue to question, transform, and embrace every facet of your being, Kindred.

This is a new beginning: A beginning filled with endless possibilities, guided by the Dark Fire, and supported by the unseen forces that walk beside you.

As sovereign beings, we step into the world not as outcasts or rebels, but as pioneers of a new way, a way that honors the depth, complexity, and beauty of our unique souls.

May your Dark Fire burn brightly, illuminating your path to sovereignty, and may you, in turn, become a beacon for those who journey through the darkness.

Together, we are transforming not just ourselves, but the very fabric of reality, weaving a new tapestry of existence where every soul is free to shine in its authentic brilliance.

Kindling Your Dark Fire: Igniting Your Path

To get you started on your journey to self-sovereignty, here are some steps to get you intimately acquainted with your own Dark Fire.

This is a combination of instinct, intuition, and deep connection with your true self and spiritual crew that will guide you as you make decisions that lead you closer to your best life.

Step 1: Introspection

The first thing I suggest is taking some quiet time for yourself and getting really honest about your life. A meditative state can be helpful here, or journaling so that you can see your thoughts and feelings laid out before you.

Where do you feel truly free to be yourself? When do you get to experience feeling authentic, free, and fulfilled? Make note of the times, places, and people these feelings happen around.

Now, be totally honest—where do you feel small, stuck, and like you're being mashed into a box so that you conform? What are the times, places, and people around which you feel most confined and drained?

These answers are likely to bring up some uncomfortable thoughts and feelings. Remember that these are all valid, and this is a time for you to honor yourself and how you truly feel.

Step 2: Identifying Your Dark Fire

This feeling of your "Dark Fire" will likely show up somewhere in your body, and this is the time for you to identify it. Lean further into all the things that make you feel activated, powerful, etc, and see what sensations come up in your body. Sit with these feelings for as long as possible so you can recognize them when they show up.

Then, go to the other end of the spectrum: think about the places, situations, and people who make you feel small and disempowered. See if this comes with its own sensation(s), and while it is uncomfortable, sit with those for a bit.

This will help you to begin recognizing your "hits" for the things that serve you, and the things that will hold you back. Keep in mind that these sensations will vary from person to person, and you may have inner voices, music, or other cues to take from.

Step 3: Small Acts

Begin choosing small things each week that kindle your Dark Fire, and lean into the sensation you get when you do these things. This will strengthen your communication with your Dark Fire and allow you to identify it (or its absence) more easily over time.

Choose to wear an outfit out that you love but have been criticized for. Say "no" to doing something you truly don't want to do but are expected to agree to. (Scandalous!) Buy or borrow a book on a topic that gives you a little thrill and makes your Dark Fire do a little dance.

Whatever feels right and literally fires up your Dark Flame, start doing it a little at a time.

Step 4: Discernment

As time goes on and you kindle those flames, you will learn more and more about how your personal Dark Fire operates. Through this process, you will strengthen your skills of discernment, and this is likely where things will begin to feel both heavy and liberating—because you will begin seeing through the B.S. that is being thrown at you every day.

You will begin to understand the layers and layers of control and programming that have been laid on you, and how many people benefit from you not changing things.

This is likely the hardest part of the whole process, because it can feel like everything you thought you knew was a lie, and you will probably lose some friends and connections over it.

Step 5: Keep Going

At this point, the best thing you can do is keep taking those small steps. Every day, one little act of rebellion will stoke your Dark Fire and forge you into an even more powerful version of yourself.

It isn't easy, but as you continue along the path that your fire has illuminated for you, you will begin to see the benefits and blessings of being in step with the person you truly came here to be.

Continuing this path is the bravest, strongest, most awe-inspiring thing you can possibly do right now.

Step 6: Embodying Your Dark Fire

You will begin to exude an unshakable confidence that will repel people who want to take advantage of you but will be magnetic to the right people. You will slowly surround yourself with others who want the same freedom and sovereignty that you have found.

You will find spiritual practices and supportive deities that will be in your pocket when you need them, and you will see things that don't serve you falling away from your life, leaving room for growth and expansion into new and wonderful things.

This is a lifelong process of embracing yourself for who you are and what you stand for. It isn't an "easy" path, but it will leave you feeling liberated and grateful to yourself for the gift of seeing yourself as the most powerful being in your own life.

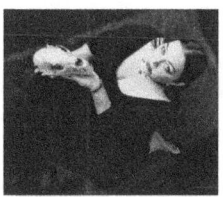

Lindsey Rainwater

Lindsey Rainwater is an author and Voidwalker here to help you recognize and embrace your own innate power. From a young age, she has been hanging out with psychopomps such as Azrael and Anubis. She's unafraid to explore the taboo, typically untouchable topics avoided by most of society. She shows people that death and rebirth are a cycle to be embraced, not just at the end of life, but in every day.

When she isn't writing or playing with yarn, you will likely not find her at all because she is camping with her "little heathens" in the mountains of Idaho.

Sign up for your free "Kindling the Dark Fire" meditation by visiting: https://stan.store/LindseyRainwater

TWENTY-TWO

Integration

Jessica Verrill

"You're too opinionated."
"You're too sensitive."
"You're too stubborn."

Or focused, persistent, loud–fill in the blank with any other adjective of power that challenges someone else or their beliefs.

For years, I shrunk myself to make others more comfortable. I was a first-class people-pleaser, chameleon, go-with-the-flow kind of lady. Pursuing personal development and healing had me listen to external voices, thinking it would help me improve myself and become more successful, happier, and healthier.

It put me in a box.

It formed cracks in the foundation of all these things in my life.

Someone else must know the way if they have what I want, or it seemed they did. I always used to remind myself not to take advice from someone you wouldn't trade places with, and yet, here I was, forming the essence of myself into something less brilliant, expansive or intelligent.

It worked–in some ways. Almost all of my former employers would likely tell you I was one of their favorite employees. I worked hard, was incredibly loyal, and would continue to show up and push

Integration

myself to be better. In my own business, I did the same. I easily connected with clients, got to know them, and made them feel comfortable while tucking away the parts of me that were raging about injustices in the world—and raging that more people weren't raging.

Without realizing the depth of it, I had silenced the "too" pieces of myself. I had silenced the opinions, the rage about injustices other people didn't seem to care about. I bit my tongue instead of speaking up. Instead of listening to myself when everything in me was saying not to focus on a certain strategy in my business, the experts pointed me in a direction, so I went.

I hustled. I learned. I pushed down my fears. I kept pushing myself forward. It was never enough. I went back to school and obtained my bachelor's of science degree. I applied to graduate school. More. I needed more. At best, I loved learning and wanted to help people better; at worst, I needed the validation that someone outside of me would give me by saying I was smart enough to have an opinion and a voice—one that needed to be respected.

Through this perpetual cycle, we become further away from our innate selves, our essence, our power, and our divinity. This certainly was the case for me. The more I tried to fit into the box, the blueprint, or the mold created by someone else, the more I felt those parts of me withering, my body along with it.

Instead of passion, I felt lackluster.

Instead of being inspired, I felt bored.

Instead of feeling joy, I felt numb.

I had achieved many things I wanted: a family, a beautiful home and a growing business with amazing clients. To my mind, I was doing it. In my heart, I knew there was more. Yet, my body was screaming the loudest. Despite my healthy habits, like eating well, exercising and regular detoxification protocols, I was steadily gaining weight. I knew something was seriously off when my naturopathic doctor recommended a hormone reset protocol, and I gained 11 pounds in 3 days, but I didn't know where else to turn or what else to look into.

Chalking it up to stress from my husband's recent health challenges with tick-borne viruses, I pushed on. After all, I was now supporting him as best I could through this, homeschooling and caring for our young child. I had just started a new publishing branch of my business and was handling almost all household needs. I was exhausted, but there was no way I could stop or put down any of the balls I was juggling.

Burnout was here. Not the, I'm tired, and I need to rest for a day, but the adrenal burn-out, crisp, fried, 'it's going to take two years to recover' type of burn-out. And still, I probably would have kept going until I found a small black thing the size of a sesame seed on my arm. If you live in the Northeast, you probably already know where this is going. A tick. Fuck.

Dutily removing it, putting it in a labeled Ziploc bag, and treating the area, taking my homeopathic Ledum, I was horrified by the thought of it coming back from the lab and testing positive for Lyme disease. My prayers were answered! It didn't come back positive–because it didn't come back. You see, in between me putting it on the counter to send out and that actually happening, my sweet girl decided to use it to put some water and sand in it, creating a little beach in the bag. Super cute, until the apprehension spread over me. The tick was gone. Which meant I would need to start a minimum regime of doxycycline, a powerful antibiotic, to be safe.

This art project turned out to be a massive blessing in disguise. Without knowing it, my daughter put me on the track needed to get my life and health back in order; it just wouldn't be quick or easy. You see when I started what should be a 30-day course of this super drug, I began having intense symptoms. Under the treatment of a Lyme-literate doctor, we decided to have some testing done, and wouldn't you know it, I was positive for a bunch of things. Lyme Disease, yep. Bartonella, that too. Babesia, sure did. Acute Epstein-Barr Virus, of course.

I believe that tick that bit me was actually negative, and had it come back from the lab with those results, I would have likely not pursued any treatment, not had such intense reactions (also known as a Herx or Herxheimer reaction) and would not have gotten to the underlying health condition that had been plaguing me for years.

Integration

While the next two years were full of many challenges, there have been many gifts. The symptoms I had were varied, including many neurological and psychological ones. I would plunge into a rage that lasted days, then switch to a darkness so deep, it made me wonder if I was going crazy while I cried continually for hours, days upon days. I developed a tremor in my hand and jaw, and I would feel like someone had turned the lights off in my brain when I was speaking, so I would lose all context of where I was or what was coming next. For a while, I had such sensitivity in my feet it hurt to walk, my body ached, I had headache upon headache, muscle twitches, insomnia, anxiety and so much more. Imagine having the worst flu you've ever had, coupled with the most devastating heartbreak, rage, anxiety and random things in your life. To say it was intense is an understatement.

My energy was minimal, but I needed to keep working, and like many business owners, you don't make money when you don't work. I had to prioritize what was most important. Every invitation and possibility was run through the filter of energetic output and the input of joy. I haven't ever been able to do anything for long that was just about the money, so it needed to fill other areas of me. For the first time, if it wasn't a hell yes or a necessity, it was a no. My boundaries got stronger. I changed my programs to involve less time in each while continuing to elevate my client offers.

As I healed my life, I healed my body.

I realized my strengths were the things I had pushed away for so long, the "too" voices. I have strong opinions because I am here to usher in change. I am not here to be a complicit, don't ask questions type of person. I question everything, and I see where things could be improved. I care. A lot. About so many things people don't even know are happening in the world. I cry because my heart feels so full. And I dig my heels in when I know I need to stand up for someone or something. Those things are beautiful. The world needs more people with conviction wanting to make an impact. We need the disrupters, the innovators, the out-of-the-box thinkers. And I came here on this earth, at this time, to be one of them.

Looking at these traits as gifts rather than a blemish to polish away has enabled me to connect more deeply with myself. What is it that I want? What am I being guided to do? How do I best serve? We aren't all the same; the sooner we embrace that, the better for everyone.

There is this tendency in our culture of healing, coaching, and therapy that we need to fix ourselves constantly.

Why?

Just because we are now conscious enough and liberated in our voices enough to say, 'These things that happened to me were not okay, and they really hurt me, changed my life, shattered my reality,' does that mean we need to spend decades dissecting every element, angle and experience of our lifetime?

No. We don't.

It is time to liberate yourself. It is time to be who you came to this world to be without apology. It starts with embracing all elements of yourself, minimizing the external voices and honoring what you are here to do with the gifts you have.

The sooner we realize our shadows or our egos are essential parts of us, the sooner we will find peace and joy.

Begin by honing your energy into the present. The more present you become, the more you can harness your power.

What sounds do you hear around you?

What can you smell?

How does your body feel? Spend some time here. There is a tendency in spiritual or personal development circles to gloss over this.

Integration

What do you see? What colors, flickers of light or shadows are in your awareness?

Can you taste anything?

Notice how this brings you back to your body, back to now. Everything is created here. Focusing on what we could, should, or would have done differently does no good, just as spending too much time in future fantasies can derail those very visions.

In this space, begin to focus on the center of your chest, your heart space. How does it feel? Are there any messages here for you?

Connect with this essence for as long as you are able. The more you become accustomed, the deeper you can go. Eventually, you may intuitively feel your soul and that of divinity more strongly. Use this for guidance or clarity, manifestation, and strengthening the power of the divine in your life.

Often, the most profound changes can be experienced in the simplest of actions. If you desire external guidance leading you back to yourself, I would be honored to support you on your journey.

With love,

Jess

Jessica Verrill

As a USA Today bestselling author and multiple-time published writer, Jessica Verrill is renowned for crafting stories that captivate hearts and ignite imaginations. As the founder of House of Indigo Publishing, she is dedicated to empowering authors to share their unique voices with the world.

With an energetic spirit and a love for adventure, Jess finds solace in the serene landscapes of Maine, where she resides with her husband, daughter and fur babies.

When not immersed in the world of writing and publishing, she can often be found exploring the great outdoors, surrounded by vibrant flowers, or lost in the pages of a captivating book. Drawn to the playful exploration of energetic realms, she constantly seeks inspiration and new avenues of creativity.

linktr.ee/jessicaverrill

Body of 9 Shadow Alchemy Appendix

The Body of 9® offers a comprehensive, body-based system to better understand ourselves and each other and context for how others see the world. We're continually informed by our physical bodies through nine distinct regions in the body that directly impact the way we experience our lives. We're each born with one of nine regions activated at birth and your life is viewed through that lens. This active region is what we at Body of 9 call your Natural Number.

Based on that active region, the body develops and presents distinct physical, intellectual, and spiritual characteristics, specifically in posture, movement, and structure, using specific muscles, bones, and fascia, and in energetic signature and purpose as well. These innate characteristics are governed by nature rather than nurture, and determine how we relate to ourselves and to others.

In nuclear families Natural Number does not repeat until you have more than seven children, as children do not inherit Natural Number from their parents until the 9 are all present. This means that in families with less than nine people, no one shares Natural Number. It is no wonder that we rarely feel seen, heard and supported in our family systems. This can impact our relationship with the *shadow* side of our Natural Number, as we may exile or hide parts of our nature to avoid unwanted attention, fit in, or conform due to a lack of felt safety or continually being told that those parts are incorrect.

Families are also smaller now than they used to be before modern medicine and industrialization; in earlier history, it was common to have families of around a dozen people, though survival rates were much lower. This means we are not exposed to all the Natural Numbers while growing up within the family. As a result, some Natural Numbers may not be as familiar or comfortable to us as the others with which we have had more experience. This may lead us to feel less prepared when we go out into the world and encounter new Natural Numbers in teachers, work colleagues and friends. Imagine how this can inform the unseen or shadow side of our worldview. It is common for people to feel ashamed, afraid, or disappointed when social interactions do not meet expectations, lead to uncomfortable situations, or even cross boundaries.

Without this ancient knowing, our parents will typically gravitate to seeing the child through their own lens instead of the child's. Unfortunately, this doesn't take into account that we are physiologically different from our parents. The result is that assumptions are made about our kids' behaviors, talents, desires and skills from the only lens of perception that we have–our own. We are influenced by culture, education, opportunity, and experience, many of which contain generations' worth of trauma, outdated information, and us-vs-them mentality. These things come together to form belief systems within us, which subtly or not-so-subtly affect parenting choices.

Each Natural Number is a perfect filtration system for the spiritual self to emerge. It is very easy to cause inadvertent harm to our loved ones, and especially children, when we apply our lens to who they are, rather than seeing their own. Without realizing it, we can shut down the gifts, the magic, and the beauty of their Natural Number and other blueprint design (Astrology, Human Design, Gene Keys, Starchetype, etc). Learning what it takes to support ourselves, our friends and family to be who they are meant to be, by their own definition, is so incredibly important.

When looked at in overall context, the wisdom of each Natural Number is easier to understand and receive as part of a greater whole.

Each Natural Number, when active, offers something entirely different from the others and shares its own unique wisdom. While each of us may identify with these gifts, they are most strongly active in those with that Natural Number. Here are the core benefits of learning each of the Natural Numbers:

• **Natural Number 1** honors others and treats them with respect, holding all equally, and providing each person with a sense of value. They help us know ourselves through creativity.

• **Natural Number 2** engages with another person as they exist in the moment, without agenda building instantaneous enlivened connection.

• **Natural Number 3** experiences the intense joy and energy of togetherness at the pure soul-level of connection, inspiring us to our greatest possibilities.

• **Natural Number 4** offers insight into self, in order to align with your core being and with others for more intimate, authentic connections.

• **Natural Number 5** helps others to become their potential, calms the mind, and reveals congruency between information and its source, whether to confirm or challenge its validity.

• **Natural Number 6** synthesizes energy available in the present moment to move a group, project, or person into action on the most alive and significant path.

- **Natural Number 7** effectively opens minds to new possibilities, instigates change, and optimizes the efficiency of these new potentials and processes.

- **Natural Number 8** uses the body to develop trust and shape integrity in ways that create safety for all. It grounds the creative process in realistic tasks and actions to manifest with integrity.

- **Natural Number 9** helps you know your place in the Universal flow, so that you can create efficiently with harmony and balance, without using excess energy or force to bring coherence.

A Deeper Dive into the Shadow & Light of Each Natural Number

Shadows in Natural Numbers come in two main forms:

1) The aligned, but shunned parts of our Nature that we hide to stay safe, and
2) The unaligned subconscious, unseen behaviors and patterns that perpetuate conflict and/or trauma.

Our goal in self-growth is to learn to embrace the aligned shadows, and work to release or repattern the unaligned or disharmonized shadows. When we can find harmony in the dance of light and shadow in life, we find ourselves far more capable of dealing with challenges, being supported, and staying self-aligned in integrity and authenticity.

All Natural Numbers are capable of sharing their profound gifts in the world when they are safe and supported to embrace their nature. These "superpowers," healthily expressed, cannot help but make a positive impact in the world and amplify authenticity, joy, harmony, and love.

While exploring the shadow aspects of each Natural Number is new work in the Body of 9 community, the more we dive in, the more we find that embracing our aligned gifts is just as important as clearing out patterns related to our disharmonized shadow-based beliefs and behaviors. Ignoring them only serves as an avoidance tactic—not a form of healing, wholeness, or integration.

We can learn to embrace the gifts or superpowers of our own and other's Natural Numbers, which is an incredible, world-altering experience. Imagine being able to literally step into someone else's shoes! But, we may also find ourselves in need of identifying and unlearning the disharmonized shadows we've picked up along the way from family members, society, peers, or partners. These misaligned behaviors were created in our own nurture, trauma, and self-repression, as well as the generations preceding us. That is why it's important to raise awareness of some of the "red flags" of internal dialogue, self-limiting beliefs, and behaviors that may indicate disharmony with the gifts of different Natural Numbers.

Within each of us is the shadow of feeling misunderstood. We long to connect and be seen in our truth: the light of who we are! It is possible! As we co-create shared language and cultivate curiosity, we can move towards greater understanding, acceptance, and even celebration of one another!

Let us clear these unaligned shadows from our communities and as a collective, embracing more of our aligned light and celebrating the uniqueness of each person!

Here is some of our current understanding of the light and shadow of each Natural Number at a very broad level. This is a very brief overview, as an entire book could be written about each Natural Number! For now, please consider this an ever-growing, non-exhaustive list of Natural Number qualities, gifts, and challenges.

Several authors in Shadow Alchemy chose to have their Natural Numbers identified as a part of the project, so we've also shared some of the Natural Number wisdom present in their chapters.

Natural Number 1

The aligned light of Natural Number 1 is about experiencing Source, where Source refers to the power of creation, the Cosmic Energy that creates life. They help us to feel, see, and share the awe, beauty and majesty of the world and the people within it. Deeply honoring and respecting others derives from this experience of Source.

The unaligned shadow of Natural Number 1 is shame and perfectionism. NN1 sees perfection in Source, and when compared to Self, they know they fall short. When not met with compassion, NN1s may shame spiral, present an illusion of perfection to others, or find themselves in deep self-judgment.

Ikenna Lughna (NN1) understands and shows us how to use our creativity as a source of connecting with our truth and overcoming perfectionism. They offer their wisdom through the lens of honoring ourselves through curiosity, compassion, and the creative process.

Tracey Peffer (NN1) experienced awe and wonder as she came into a deeper relationship with her intuition. These profound experiences led her to share her findings and gifts with others so that they, too, can honor their own unique nature and connection with Source.

Natural Number 2

The aligned light of Natural Number 2 is about connection through relationships to the magic in others. It is a merging with others, attuning with our whole being to the body of another person for the sake of connection alone. Natural Number 2 teaches us that everything starts with a connection through active engagement and movement.

The unaligned shadows of Natural Number 2 are disappointment in self and others, neglecting their own needs, and fear of expectations. They can become swallowed, losing their voice and power, by mirroring others completely. They may not be able to step into their own light, while it is easy for them to see it in others.

There were no identified Natural Number 2 authors in this book.

Natural Number 3

The aligned light of Natural Number 3 is about a focused connection to others that ignores the persona and goes straight to our being, our greater purpose. They use the joy of connection from that relationship to inspire us into action toward that purpose. As heralds of our being, they announce our purpose to the universe so that we may be included in the universal plan of manifestation and creation.

Natural Number 3's greatest shadow is fear: fear of anger, judgment, their own power, and imperfection. They may struggle with leaning into bliss completely or connecting as deeply as they can with others, as they fear an imperfect soul connection with another. The belief that "It's not perfect" can cause shadows to arise. NN3 may fear showing up with the full intensity of their energy, joy, and focus and so dampen who they are to fit in with expectations.

There were no identified Natural Number 3 authors in this book.

Natural Number 4

The aligned light of Natural Number 4 is about our relationship to our infinite self, to our life-force within our being. Through knowing and accepting our timeless selves, we are ready to transform using our connection to our deepest life force energy. From there we find a place of alignment and authenticity.

For Natural Number 4, the unaligned shadow is often outside, as they access their emotions and consciousness within the aligned shadow deep within. Natural Number 4 may retreat when the world is disappointing. When outside circumstances do not align with their authentic purpose, safety, and energy, they may believe something is wrong with them and the world around them. This may cause them to completely "vanish" from social circles as they go within to puzzle out their experience.

Michelle Hamady (NN4) shares her profound relationship with shadows and the wisdom in her emotions. Unafraid to go within, she beautifully illustrates our capacity to process the darkest of circumstances and still find the light of the inner child present within us.

Raeleen Castle (NN4) expresses how impactful it has been for her to take time to go within, feel, and process her shadows.

Through ritual and writing, she finds flow and freedom, allowing her to surrender to her fullest authentic expression and invite others to do the same.

Natural Number 5

Natural Number 5 sets and holds the context for transformation—what do we know, what do we need to find out, how is what we know related to everything else and what are the relationships between people, knowledge and intuition that need to be understood? Natural Number 5s know that everything is interconnected, knowable and needs to be congruent in order to be accepted into the existing framework of understanding.

The unaligned shadow of Natural Number 5 is shame and withdrawal from community. NN5 may strive to do everything on their own, from their own knowing, to the point of misaligned independence. They may find themselves frustrated with others' limited views. They may also struggle to share their own needs, neglecting their emotions and needs while helping others.

Kristine McPeak (NN5) is a collector of tools and knowledge that can assist just about anyone in moving through their challenges. She is eager to help others find the information that will most empower them to understand themselves. Her chapter beautifully showcases the interconnectedness of past and present, which, when brought together, can yield a more self-congruent future.

Natural Number 6

The aligned light of Natural Number 6 points us in the most alive direction, providing the energy necessary for movement on the universal path to overcome any inherent inertia. Natural Number 6s experience the energy present in a situation, they decode and magnify it back, so that everyone can tap into the energy of the moment.

When unaligned shadow is present, Natural Number 6s often find themselves in battle with fear–as powerful manifestors, they may manifest what they are trying to avoid. They may fear not being loved, being smothered, or being alone. They may find themselves holding their breath. As their gift is seeing the aliveness in any given moment, they may fear or look away from the unseen or unalive content of the world, often associated with the shadow.

Susan Fisher (NN6) explores her own experiences of "aliveness" in energy throughout her life, and how each of these moments of challenge or growth brought her closer to her purpose. She now magnifies the impact of this ancient wisdom in her work through Body of 9®, helping others overcome their own blockages and reunite with their bodies so they can live presently and with awareness.

Kim Paget (NN6) speaks to the hard truths of the "fairytales" we grew up with that are not helpful for us or our communities. Her direct, no-nonsense energy is evident in her words as she invites all of us to be accountable and empowered so that we can get real with what is right for us!

In her dynamic screenplay-like chapter, Kelly Mowers (NN6) addresses the challenges of judgment and loss, bringing life to her words through poetry and monologue. She explores her truth in juxtaposition with what others expected of her, expressing the need for healthy communities, powerful inner presence and alignment.

Natural Number 7

In the aligned light, Natural Number 7 is about change, purpose, and possibility. NN7 sees optimized possibilities and purpose of a person, group, or community, and they can present a path and options that have not yet been envisioned that will move those involved toward their greatest purpose. They also enable us to leave behind that which no longer serves us to ensure that we can move forward toward our great vision and stay open to what we do not yet know. Change is inherent in transformation; NN7 helps us let go of what no longer serves, thereby creating space to open to new possibilities.

The unaligned shadow of Natural Number 7 may look like frustration and shame if their messages and delivery of truth is not valued by those around them. They may have a self-care imbalance, move between high and low energy, or find themselves rejecting life without purpose. NN7s are extraordinarily vulnerable–misaligned shadows are felt in equal extremes as their beacon of light. NN7 may feel shame around their emotions and find themselves caught up in their heads, overthinking.

Sara Giza (NN7) knows that it is possible to reclaim our personal power and autonomy, even after intense trauma. She recognizes the importance of processing our experiences so that we can let them go and move toward the divine perfection in each of us. She shares the truth that when we can find the gifts in our shadows, we feel more whole and self-aligned.

Dawn Sullivan (NN7) shares her recognition of how we can step into the best possible version of ourselves. This takes work! When her ego desired to say "No," she found the "Yes" available to her, leaning into art, retreat, and her own infinite wisdom to embrace her full self and potential. She demonstrates this is something we can choose to do, for the good of ourselves and the world.

Natural Number 8

Natural Number 8 guides us to move forward together to create with consideration and integrity for the benefit of all. Aligning the body with the physical source of creation, the earth, they draw energy into their body. Their body guides them to create an atmosphere ripe for growth and healing where safety and support are fully present. NN8 teaches the gift of boundaries, and they have a natural energetic shield.

The unaligned shadow of Natural Number 8 can look like loss of physical connection to the body, withdrawal from others to attempt to alleviate pain, and pushing to override their body, causing physical harm. It may be extremely challenging for a NN8 to draw boundaries with someone once they've already been let in beyond their shield. NN8s may hide deep disappointments with others and find themselves testing relationships.

Xeres Villanueva (NN8) shares the challenges that come when our bodily integrity and safety are compromised. She highlights the importance of self-advocacy and listening to our bodies' needs each step of our journey. Her perspectives help us understand how we must honor what our bodies feel, how they respond, and our needs as we move through the healing process.

Natural Number 9

In the aligned light, Natural Number 9 appears as harmony and balance. Natural Number 9 holds the container for everything that exists: all shadow and all light. They recognize when to begin transformation and change processes, and when to bring completion which releases the energy to create again. NN9 understands how to include everything, create unity, and shepherd our human experience through the transformation process. They live within all that is, making their experience completely expansive. None of the other Natural Numbers contain everything; this makes it hard for others to comprehend the breadth and perceive the impact of Natural Number 9.

The unaligned shadow of Natural Number 9 looks like existential overwhelm, fear, and freeze. When reaching the point of critical awareness of physical reality, everything becomes too big to balance, so they retreat inside (or beyond) to regain a sense of balance: it may be effortless to leave the body behind. They may fear causing waves so much that they freeze completely, overloaded with the expansive possibilities for chaos or negative ripple effects. Feeling misunderstood, scapegoated, and not standing up for themselves may also be disharmonized NN9 shadows.

Both Jess Verrill and Safrianna Lughna, who co-facilitated the creation of this book, have Natural Number 9. Often with Natural Number 9s we are not sure how things are getting done, but they do. Their picture is so big, and their method so gentle that we do not perceive the growth and change they cultivate.

Jess Verrill (NN9) explores her expansive view of humanity and the self in her writing, addressing how society often puts us in boxes. When we break free, we embrace our strengths and allow ourselves to be as we are through compassionate self-acceptance. Jess shares the most important and simple thing we can do: come back to ourselves.

As publisher and co-leader, Jess guided and supported the

overall energetic balance and flow of the book, project, and community, creating a container where each author could thrive and be supported throughout each step and beyond. In providing the layout and design vision for the book, she ultimately brought about the birth of the manuscript!

Safrianna Lughna (NN9) shares the magic felt within her natural center of leadership through her descriptions of her "wings." She explores the concept of shadow and light as two halves of the same force that moves us toward flight. Even though life is a constant series of healing rebirths, Safrianna holds the vision that all things can be integrated as we learn to flow, forgive, and lead with compassion.

As lead editor and co-leader, Safrianna held the big picture for the manuscript, helping guide each author to authentically express their voice and share their wisdom for an ultimately uplifting experience.

Red MoonEagle has an incredible level of self-mastery in her body. When she was first identified, it was challenging to pinpoint her Natural Number. In the context of her chapter, this makes even more sense as she has navigated the "deaths" of the body's centers of activation throughout her lifetime. However, Red's voice and perspective in this book express that of Natural Number 9: containing the entire picture of the universe with and without her body.

The Wisdom of All Numbers Working Together Creates Harmonized Communities

The gifts of each Natural Number cannot serve in their highest potential without a community to offer them to. Community is not safe and stable without the recognition that each and every one of us has authenticity to share. When conformity is pushed as the norm, and harmful, pejorative labels or stereotypes are placed upon people routinely.

We must stop re-traumatizing ourselves and each other with our unaligned, unseen shadows. We heal ourselves and others through self-ownership. Shining a light into the seemingly scary shadows, especially with support, often reveals that they are not nearly as scary as we may have thought. We are empowered when we're willing to go within and reclaim the gifts we've abandoned, and also recognize where we may be in self-sabotage, unconscious incompetence, or cycles of shame, fear, or disappointment.

Allow yourself the gift of self-awareness. See how you belong within yourself and in community. Celebrate how you contribute to the world and own your power. Get curious about yourself, light, shadow, and all! Get curious about others and how they offer similar or complimentary gifts to the world. Celebrate your one-of-a-kind nature alongside the shared language and understanding you can use to connect with others.

You are whole!

Appendix Co-Created by Susan Bennett Fisher, Safrianna Lughna, and Red MoonEagle as a part of their ongoing study and development of The Body of 9®

HOUSE OF INDIGO

About the Publisher

House of Indigo, a boutique publishing house, was created to give authors the platform to share the beauty and truth of their experiences and wisdom, without censorship or dilution.

We believe our stories, and vision have great power to make an impact within the consciousness of the world. Through stories, we forge connections that bridge the gaps between us, gaining deeper insights into each other's lives.

At the heart of our mission lies an unwavering commitment to excellence in every facet of our productions and service. We meticulously curate each project with an uncompromising dedication to quality, ensuring that every story we share resonates with our energetic integrity and standards.

For more information: Houseofindigocollective.com

www.ingramcontent.com/pod-product-compliance
Lightning Source LLC
Chambersburg PA
CBHW071656160426
43195CB00012B/1491